Ninja Foodi Cookbook

The Complete Ninja Foodi Pressure Cooker Cookbook with Fast and Flavorful Recipes for Weight Loss & Healthy Life

Jen Andreev

© Copyright 2020 By Jen Andreev All Right Reserved.

In no way it is legal to reproduce, duplicate, or transmit any part of this document by other electronic means or printed format. Any recording of this publication is strictly prohibited, and any storage of this material is not allowed unless with a written permission from the publisher. All rights reserved.

The information provided herein is stated to be truthful and consistent, in that any liability, regarding inattention or otherwise, by any use or abuse of any policies, processes, or directions contained within is the solitary and complete responsibility of the recipient reader. Under no circumstances will any legal liability or blame be held against the publisher for any reparation, damages, or monetary loss due to the information herein, either directly or indirectly.

Legal Notice:

This book is copyright protected. This is only for personal use. You cannot amend, distribute, sell, use, quote or paraphrase any part or the content within this book without the consent of the author or copyright owner. Legal action will be pursued if it is breached

DISCLAIMER NOTICE:

Please only read the information contained within this document is for educational purposes only. Every attempt has been made to provide accurate, up to date, complete and reliable information. No warranties of any kind are expressed or implied. Readers acknowledge that the author is not engaged in the rendering of legal, financial, medical or professional advice.

By reading this document, the reader agrees that under no circumstances are we responsible for any losses, direct or indirect, which are incurred as a result of the use of information contained in this document, including but not limited to errors, omissions, or any inaccuracies

Table of Content

INTRODUCTION 8

    Ninja Foodie Pressure Cooker Basics 9
    Benefits of Ninja Foodi Pressure cooker 11
    Different types of models: 12

CHAPTER 1: BEEF, PORK AND LAMB RECIPES 13

    Recipe 1: Ninja Foodi Baby Back Ribs 15
    Recipe 2: Ninja Foodi Flank Steak 17
    Recipe 3: Thai Roast Beef 19
    Recipe 4: Beef Meat loaf 21
    Recipe 5: Ninja Foodi Stir Fry beef 23
    Recipe 6: Ground Beef with Acorn squash 25
    Recipe 7: Beef Fajitas 27
    Recipe 8: Beef Curry 29
    Recipe 9: Curried Beef Liver 31
    Recipe 10: Ninja Foodi Lamb with Orange 33
    Recipe 11: Pork with peaches 35
    Recipe 112: Pulled Pork 37
    Recipe 13: Pork Carnitas 39
    Recipe 14: Stuffed Pork Chops 41

CHAPTER 2: DESSERT, BREAD AND ROLL RECIPES 43

    Recipe 15: Ninja Foodi Chocolate Cake 45
    Recipe 16: Apple Cobbler 47
    Recipe 17: Banana Cinnamon cake 49
    Recipe 18: Chocolate Cupcakes 51
    Recipe 19: Cherry and Chocolate Frosted Cake 53
    Recipe 20: Chocolate Cheesecake 55
    Recipe 21: Chocolate Fondant 57
    Recipe 22: Orange and cherry cake 59
    Recipe 23: Homemade Bread 61
    Recipe 24: Sourdough Bread 63
    Recipe 25: Flat bread with cheese 65
    Recipe 26: Pumpkin Bread 66
    Recipe 27: Non Knead Bread 68
    Recipe 28: Zucchini Bread 70
    Recipe 29: Soda Bread 71
    Recipe 30: Cashew Bread 73
    Recipe 31: Nuts Bread 75

Recipe 32: Dates Bread ... 77
Recipe 33: Focaccia Bread ... 79
Recipe 34: Carrot and Orange Bread ... 81
Recipe 35: Ninja Foodi No Yeast Bread ... 82
Recipe 36: Wonton Rolls ... 84
Recipe 37: Chicken Wontons ... 85
Recipe 38: Cheese Chips ... 87

CHAPTER 3: SOUP AND STEW RECIPES ... 88

Recipe 39: Pumpkin Soup ... 90
Recipe 40: Cream Soup with bacon ... 91
Recipe 41: Celeriac Soup ... 93
Recipe 42: Chicken and vegetables Soup ... 95
Recipe 43: Beef stew ... 97
Recipe 44: Pork Stew ... 98
Recipe 45: Lamb Stew ... 100
Recipe 46: Tomato soup ... 101
Recipe 47: Artichoke Soup ... 103
Recipe 48: Blacked Eye Pea Stew ... 105
Recipe 49: Potato Soup ... 107
Recipe 50: Broccoli Soup ... 109
Recipe 51: Lentil and carrots Soup ... 111
Recipe 52: Mushroom Soup ... 113
Recipe 53: Spicy Chili ... 115
Recipe 54: Shrimp Stew ... 117
Recipe 55: Quinoa Stew ... 119
Recipe 56: Shrimp Angel Pasta ... 123
Recipe 57: Ground Beef Spaghetti ... 125
Recipe 58: Cheesy Pasta ... 127
Recipe 59: Ninja Foodi Spicy Pepperoni Pasta with Cheese ... 129
Recipe 60: Ninja Foodi Lasagne ... 130
Recipe 61: Ninja Foodi Gnocchi ... 132
Recipe 62: Ninja Meatball Pasta ... 134
Recipe 63: Ninja Foodi Chicken Ramen ... 136
Recipe 64: Vermicelli Rice Noodles ... 138
Recipe 65: Pasta Salad ... 140
Recipe 66: Ninja Foodi Cannelloni ... 142
Recipe 67: Ninja Foodi Pepperoni Pasta ... 144
Recipe 68: Ninja Foodi Fettuccini ... 146
Recipe 69: Beef Wellington ... 148
Recipe 70: Tuna Fusilli ... 150
Recipe 71: Ninja Foodi Mac and Cheese ... 151
Recipe 72: Stuffed Pasta Shells with cheese and tomato sauce ... 153

Recipe 73: Seafood Pasta 155
Recipe 74: Pasta Bolognese 157
Recipe 75: Ninja Foodi Picadillo 159

CHAPTER 5: STAPLE RECIPES 161

Recipe 77: Ninja Foodi Stuffed Okra 165
Recipe 78: Ninja foodi Donuts...167
Recipe 79: Ninja Foodi Biscuits 169
Recipe 80: Butter Fingers 171
Recipe 81: Peach Cake 173
Recipe 82: Pineapple Cobbler..175
Recipe 83: Ninja Foodi Bluberry Cobbler 177
Recipe 84: Caramel Cobbler 179
Recipe 85: Marshmallow Pudding 181
Recipe 86: Ninja Foodi Scones 183
Recipe 87: Ninja Foodi Pikelets 185
Recipe 88: Anzac Biscuits 187
Recipe 89: Chocolate Madeleine 189
Recipe 90: Snow balls...191
Recipe 91: Palmier Biscuits..193
Recipe 92: Ninja Foodi Croissant 195
Recipe 93: Catucini Biscuits 197
Recipe 94: Cocoa-Dusted Biscuits..199
Recipe 95: Cherry Soufflé 201
Recipe 96: Ninja Foodi Tiramisu 203
Recipe 97: Rolled Oats and carrots bars 205
Recipe 98: Fruit Tart 207
Recipe 99: Stuffed Baked Apples 210
Recipe 100: Crumbled Apple..212

CONCLUSION: 214

INTRODUCTION

It is all in one; a multi-cooker that acts as an air fryer, a pressure cooker and a slow cooker at the same time. Any Ninja Foodi is equipped with a built-in crisping element. So, if you are looking forward to try the newest revolutionary cooking appliance, then you have come to the right place and you have knocked the right door. Welcome to the newest all-in-one game changing multi-cooker that you will become obsessed to right from the first use. This guide to the Ninja Cooking use comes with 100 mesmerizing recipes tested by experienced cooks.

The large array of 100 recipes you will find in this Ninja Foodi cookbook offers you pressure cooking, slow-cooking and air-frying recipes from breakfast to different types of snacks, appetizers and various categories of dishes that will invite your buds and invite you to indulge in one of a kind cooking experience.

Friendly and approachable; you will find that this cookbook, not only offers you a wide range of recipes, starting from different types of meats to breads and even desserts, to staples; but it will also provide you with all the necessary information you need to learn about the Ninja Foodi. You will find the guidance you need to make your favourite Air Fried fish and chips; as well as other crispy recipes.

And if you are wondering if you can make your favourite Mac and cheese, and even chicken fingers, you will be able to prepare it without any delay. Taquitos, tacos, even crème brûlée, crispy food, tender meals and even slow cooked dishes; it is all possible with the help of Ninja Foodi. In this cookbook, you will find something for everyone in this easy-to use book.

Furthermore, the Ninja Foodi cooking appliance paces to help you create a game-changing cooking journey you have never experienced and enjoyed like before. Besides, you will be able to discover an innovative cooking style with the help of just a few buttons.

Once you use Ninja Foodi just for a few times, you will discover how simple and easy-to master it is. And while cooking any dish will take a lot of time and preparations to get your meal served on the table; the Ninja Foodi will do it all for you as this cooking appliances, air crisps, bakes, broils, roasts, slow-cooks and does different cooking options for you all with the same cooking appliance.

The Ninja Foodi stands out from various cooking appliance in style as well as in performance. Besides, Ninja Foodies allow you to replace countertop appliances, including slow cookers, multi-cookers, air fryers and stovetop pressure cookers; besides, every Ninja Foodi is equipped with a multi use pot that will make your cooking journey easier.

So, in a few words, the main objective of Ninja Foodi is to create some flawless dishes that you can offer to your friends and beloved ones. And even if you are a beginner to the world of Ninja Foodies, there is nothing you can't do with this revolutionary cooking appliance. So, if you have already purchased a Ninja Foodi, and you don't know how to use it or where to start from, this is the right place to start from. Now, with this Foodi at your side and this book on your bookshelf; you will be able to Ninja Cook like a pro.

Ninja Foodie Pressure Cooker Basics

The Ninja Foodi Cooker is a versatile cooking machine that works as a pressure cooker, air fryer and that grills, steams, roasts, air fries, bakes and roast at the same time. Besides, using a Ninja Foodi, you can get frozen meat in just 20 minutes. And when you finish, the ceramic pot can be easily cleaned in a dishwasher. But before using Ninja Foodi, there are some tips and using basics that you have to know beforehand:

- **The "Pressure" function button:**

You can use hot water when pressure cooking so that it can help the Ninja Foodi build pressure within faster.

- **The "Steam" function button:**

With the button "Steam", you can add another layer of texture to your steamed vegetables. And all that you need to do is to steam any ingredient you want in the Cook and Crisp Basket; then toss with the oil and Air Crisp afterwards with the Air Crisping lid on.

- **Using the Sear/Sauté function:**

Just like using a stovetop; you should use the LOW setting function for simmering and the MED button for sautéing; while you should use HI for searing or boiling meals or any type of meats. And whenever you sear meats; just leave it at room temperature for about 20 to 30 minutes; then pat dry before searing it to obtain best results. You can use the "Sear" button before slow cooking or pressure cooking to help build a better caramelization and flavors in your meals.

- **Air Crisp function**

When using Ninja Foodies, it is required to evenly coat your vegetables with a little of oil before air crisping it. Indeed, this will help achieve a high level of crispiness. All you have to do is to arrange ingredients as evenly as possible in the Cook and Crisp Basket.

- **Broil function**

The broiling function can be used as a second phase in Ninja Foodi combo-cooking recipes and it can finish off your meals with a crispy taste. But don't forget to sneak even a small peek throughout the cooking process so that you can check the crispiness of your foods.

- **The "Keep Warm" Function:**

This specific function can be used on its own in a way that it will keep your ingredients at a food-safe temperature and it is great for ingredients like dips and pulled pork.

- **The Function button "dehydrator":**

Vegetables and fruits should always be patted as dry as you can before placing it into your Cook and Crisp Basket. All you have to do is to place the ingredients in the basket and close together;

but make sure to overlap pieces or stack it. Most of the fruits and the different types of veggies take about 6 to 8 hours to be dehydrated, while the jerky takes about 5 to 7 hours. And the longer you dehydrate your ingredients, the crispier they will become. To finish off any types of dehydrated meats and fish, we recommend using the function "Roast" at a temperature of about 330°F.

Benefits of Ninja Foodi Pressure cooker

Have you ever felt curious about the combination device Ninja Foodi, which includes at the same time, air fryer, pressure cooker and slow cooker? Having a Ninja Foodi Pressure cooker as an indispensable part of your food preparation equipment offers you several advantages. And here are some of the most important benefits of using Ninja Foodies:

1. **Ninja Foodies combine two used devices in just one device:**

2. **Having a Ninja Foodi, you don't have to move your hot food around**

Possessing a Ninja Foodi, pressure cooker air fryer means that you don't have to move your hot food from a pressure cooker to Air Fryers. So using a Ninja Foodi is safer for you to use than any cooking appliance.

3. **Less storage than using two devices:**

Ninja Foodi is a large pressure cooking and air frying device; hereby, we can say that Ninja Foodi includes two devices at the same time. And even though Ninja foodi includes two devices in just one, it will take up less room than two devices would do. And this can be really convenient for dorm rooms, small kitchens and for people who love to travels, this device can fit everywhere in your travelling bag.

4. **Ninja Foodi is easy-to clean**

Ninja Foodi is very easy-to clean, which makes a great plus for you. And being easy-to clean; makes Ninja Foodies a device that is efficient and this major makes a key that encourages us to use it.

5. **The function Bake/Roast:**

In addition to working as a pressure cooker, a steamer, dehydrator, slow cooker and air fryer; this device is also considered is also a small portable addition to serving as a pressure cooker, an air fryer, a steamer, and a slow cooker, this device is also considered as a small portable oven. So you can bake whatever you want in a Ninja Foodi.

6. **Saves energy**

Ninja Foodi Pressure Cookers can be more efficient than any other cooking appliances and it can result in important energy saving. And this cooking gadget lends itself, not only to one-pot cooking recipes, but also to air fried recipes. And since recipes require less time to cook with the help of a Ninja Foodi, it consumes less energy and that is all that any of us wants.

Different types of models:

If cooking at home is something new thing for you, using a Ninja Foodi can greatly help you. Not only Ninja Foodi can help save your time, and counter space, but it will also enable you to cook some of the most delicious recipes you can ever taste.

The Ninja Foodi is a multi-cooker, a pressure cooker and an Air fryer at the same time. And this cooking appliance is the only pressure and multi cooker that is equipped with this capability. So if you are looking for a cooking appliance that focuses on air frying function, and that can save you time and energy; Ninja Foodies make a great choice for you.

Even more importantly, Ninja Foodies can help make you look better and cook better. But before making your first Ninja Foodi purchase, you should know which type of Ninja Foodies you should use, otherwise you will feel lost in front of the various and different brands of Ninja Foodies that you will find available.

1. **Ninja OP301 Pressure Cooker, Steamer and Air Fryer**

The price of this brand of Ninja Foodi varies between $200 and $250. And this is the best air frying and pressure cooking unit at the same time in just one unit. This cooking appliance will allow you to cook your favorite stews, chili, desserts, casseroles, snacks and chili to perfection.

2. **Ninja Foodi 8-in-1 Digital Toaster SP101**

The price of this model of Ninja is estimated at about $210 to $250. And the Ninja Foodi 8-in-1 Digital toaster is more efficient than you expect it. And this energy-saving and space-saving cooking gadget can also air roast, air fry, dehydrate, air broil and keep you food warm.

3. **Ninja Foodi Tender-Crisp Pressure Cooker OP300**

The price of this cooking appliance is estimated by $179 to $229. The Ninja Foodi is a pressure cooker and air fryer in just one appliance. So, you can pressure cook a whole chicken; then you can crisp its skin using the same appliance.

4. **Ninja Multi-Cooker with 4-in-1 Stove Top, Oven, Steam and Slow Cooker Options, 6-Quart Non-stick Pot, and Steaming/Roasting Rack (MC950Z), Black:**

Ninja Foodi is a pot that is equipped with 4 cooking functions: Slow Cook, Steam, stove Top. And unique heating elements can help you sauté, slow cook and sear all in just one pot for clean up. Learn how to steam healthy and delicious vegetables, fish and any other types of delicate foods of about 6 qt

CHAPTER 1: BEEF, PORK AND LAMB RECIPES

Recipe 1: Ninja Foodi Baby Back Ribs

TIME TO PREPARE
10 minutes

COOK TIME
25 Minutes

SERVING
3-4 People

Ingredients

- 1 slab of baby back ribs
- 1 teaspoon of grated ginger
- 1 minced scallion
- ½ tbsp of chopped cilantro
- 1 small seeded and chopped jalapeño
- 1 minced clove of garlic
- 1 cup of orange juice
- 2 tbsp of sesame oil

Instructions

1. Put your ingredients inside a plastic bag overnight. Reserve the marinade.
2. Place the ribs in a vertical manner in the Air Crisp basket of your Ninja Foodi.
3. Slide the Air Crisp basket in your Ninja Foodi.
4. Select the setting Air Crisp
5. Set the timer to around 20 minutes and the temperature to 365° F.
6. Meanwhile, put the marinade in a deep cooking pan.
7. Cook the marinade over a moderate heat for 5 minutes.
8. When the cooking time is finally complete, brush your ribs with the marinade you have prepared.
9. Select the setting SEAR/SAUTE and sauté for about 6 additional minutes
10. Cut the ribs; then serve it together with the marinade.
11. Enjoy your dish!

Nutrition Information

Calories: 290 | Fat: 20g | Carbohydrates: 20 g | Fiber: 0g | Protein: 25g

Recipe 2: Ninja Foodi Flank Steak

TIME TO PREPARE
7 minutes

COOK TIME
18 Minutes

SERVING
3-4 People

Ingredients

- 1 lb of thinly sliced flank steak
- 1 tsp of minced and grated fresh ginger
- 2 tsp of minced garlic
- 2 tsp of olive oil
- ½ cup of soy sauce
- ½ cup of water or beef broth
- ¼ cup of rice wine vinegar
- 2 tbsp of brown sugar
- 1 bag of frozen broccoli florets, about 10oz
- 2 tbsp of cornstarch dissolved into about ¼ cup of water

Instructions

1. Place the steak, the ginger, the garlic, and the oil into the bottom of your Ninja Foodi pressure cooker insert
2. Turn on your Ninja foodi on the setting sauté; then use the brown/sear on the Ninja Foodi
3. Cook for about 8 minutes or until the meat is no longer pink; then turn off the setting function sauté
4. Stir in the soy sauce, the broth, the vinegar and the brown sugar.
5. Close the lid and the steam valve; then set to High Pressure for about 5 minutes
6. Do a quick release method when the timer beeps; then lift the lid.
7. Add the frozen broccoli into your Ninja Foodi pot and set to the function sauté again with the lid open.
8. Slowly stir until the broccoli is perfectly cooked.
9. In a medium bowl; whisk the cornstarch, about 5 tbsp of hot liquid from until the mixture is smooth
10. Add into the Ninja Pot and let thicken
11. Turn off the pot; then serve alone or with rice

12. Serve and enjoy your dish!

Nutrition Information

Calories: 187| Fat: 6g | Carbohydrates: 9 g | Fiber: 1g |Protein: 21g

Recipe 3: Thai Roast Beef

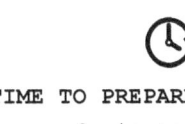

TIME TO PREPARE
6 minutes

COOK TIME
15 Minutes

SERVING
3 People

Ingredients

- 1 lb of top side beef meat
- 1 tbsp of olive oil
- 1 pinch of salt
- 1 pinch of black pepper
- For the salad: Take 2 grated carrots, ½ medium grated white cabbage, 1 finely sliced red pepper, 1 pinch of sugar snap peas, 1 pinch of bean sprouts and 1 tbsp of toasted sesame seeds with 1 small bunch of coriander leaves that are chopped (remember to keep some aside for garnish)
- For dressing your dish: 2 tbsp of fish sauce+ 2

Instructions

1. Preheat your Ninja Foodi to its maximum temperature for about 3 minutes by pressing the button SEAR/SAUTE
2. Meanwhile, prepare the beef meat.
3. Rub the beef with oil, the salt and the pepper.
4. Place the beef in the Air Crisp Basket and place the Air Crisp basket in the Ninja Foodi and close the lid
5. Set the timer to about 12 minutes and the temperature to 390°F using the button AIR CRISP
6. Meanwhile, prepare your salad by mixing all the ingredients together and leave it aside.
7. Now place the ingredients in a food blender and blitz it for 1 minute.
8. Drizzle some of the dressing over the salad.
9. Once the meat is perfectly roasted, remove it and set it aside for 20 minutes.
10. Cut the meat into slices and serve it with the salad.
11. Garnish your meat with coriander, peanuts and you can also add lime wedges.
12. Serve and enjoy an amazing dish!

tbsp of fresh lime juice+ 2 red chillies+ 2 cloves of garlic+ 1 pinch of ginger powder + 2 tbsp of tamari or soy sauce+ 2 tbsp of sesame oil
- 4 tbsp of water
- 1 tbsp of brown sugar.
- 3 chopped shallots
- 1 Pinch of salt

Nutrition Information

Calories: 341.3| Fat: 9.8g | Carbohydrates: 33.1 g | Fiber: 2g |Protein: 29.1g

Recipe 4: Beef Meat loaf

TIME TO PREPARE
7 minutes

COOK TIME
10 Minutes

SERVING
7 People

Ingredients

- 1½ lb of ground beef
- 1 beaten egg
- ½ teaspoon of Dijon mustard
- ½ cup of ketchup
- 1 medium Chopped onion
- ½ Chopped of red pepper
- ½ Cup of organic cream
- 1and ½ teaspoon of sea salt
- ½ cup of oats
- 1 cup of buttered sprouted grain toast
- 1and ½ tablespoons of sugar
- ½ of ketchup
- 3 tbsp of cane sugar

Instructions

1. Mix your ingredients all together in a bowl
2. Form a loaf out of the meat mixture
3. Place the loaf on a baking sheet in your Air Crisp basket
4. Place the baking sheet in the Air Crisp basket in your Ninja Foodi
5. Set the temperature to about 350° F
6. Spoon the toppings over the Loaf
7. Cook the loaf in the Ninja Foodi for about 10 minutes.
8. Slice the meatloaf; then serve and enjoy it!

- 2 teaspoons of ground mustard
- ½ teaspoon of chilli powder

Nutrition Information

Calories: 250| Fat: 16g | Carbohydrates: 12 g | Fiber: 1g |Protein: 14g

Recipe 5: Ninja Foodi Stir Fry beef

TIME TO PREPARE
5 minutes

COOK TIME
10 Minutes

SERVING
3-4 People

Ingredients

- 1 Pound of cut into flank steak, cut into strips
- ½ Cup of snow peas
- ½ Cup of shredded carrots
- ½ Cup of broccoli
- ½ Cup of sliced red onions
- For the Beef Marinade:
- ¼ cup of hoisin sauce
- 2 teaspoons of minced garlic
- 1 teaspoon of sesame oil
- 1 tablespoon of soy sauce
- 1 teaspoon of ground ginger
- ¼ cup of water

Instructions

1. Start by plugging in the Ninja Foodi; then press the start button, SEAR/SAUTE
2. Add in the oil and wait for about 30 seconds
3. Add in the beef, the vegetables, and the sauce to the Ninja Foodi
4. Close the lid of your Ninja Foodi and set the timer for about 10 minutes using the button "Pressure"
5. Make sure the valve is in sealed position
6. When the pressure cooking time is up; do a quick release pressure
7. Serve and enjoy your dish!

Nutrition Information

Calories: 110| Fat: 5g | Carbohydrates: 15 g | Fiber: 2g |Protein: 3g

Recipe 6: Ground Beef with Acorn squash

TIME TO PREPARE
5 minutes

COOK TIME
11 Minutes

SERVING
3 People

Ingredients

- ½ cup of cooked ground beef
- ½ cup of cooked quinoa
- 1 baked acorn squash
- ½ cup of chopped onion
- 1 tbsp of extra coconut oil
- ¼ cup of currants
- ¼ cup of sunflower seeds
- 1-2 minced garlic cloves
- 1 teaspoon of dried basil
- 1 teaspoon of sea salt

Instructions

1. Place the acorn squash in the Air Crisp Basket and place the basket in the Ninja foodi
2. Cut the squash in halves and toss into the Air Crisp Basket; then close the Ninja Foodi with a lid and press the button "Air Crisp"; and air crisp for about 10 minutes at a temperature of about 360°F
3. Remove the squash from the Ninja Foodi
4. Bake the seeds in an oven until they become crunchy
5. Meanwhile, place your ground beef with the quinoa in the pressure cooker insert
6. Sauté the onion in the coconut oil and sauté for about 6 minutes using the setting button "SEAR/SAUTE"
7. Add in the currants, the sunflower seeds, the garlic, the basil, the salt, the cumin and the paprika.
8. Stir very well until the ingredients are combined.
9. Place half of the mixture you have obtained in each

- ½ teaspoon of cumin
- ½ teaspoon of paprika

half of the acorn squash.
10. Serve and enjoy your dish!

Nutrition Information

Calories: 424.5| Fat: 7.9g | Carbohydrates: 58.3 g | Fiber: 8.2g |Protein: 30.8g

Recipe 7: Beef Fajitas

TIME TO PREPARE
4-5 minutes

COOK TIME
10 Minutes

SERVING
3 People

Ingredients

- 2 lb of beef, cut into thin strips
- 6 tbsp of coconut oil
- ½ cup of lemon or lime juice
- 4 peeled and mashed garlic cloves
- ½ teaspoon of chilli powder
- 1 seeded and sliced red pepper
- 1 yellow seeded and sliced pepper
- 2 medium thinly sliced onions
- Coconut oil
- 12 tortillas
- 2 tbsp of melted butter

Instructions

1. Prepare a combination of oil and lemon or lime juice
2. Add the spices and mix the ingredients very well with beef meat.
3. Marinate for 5 hours.
4. Remove the marinated mixture from the fridge and pat dry the meat.
5. Take the Air Crisp basket of the Ninja Foodi and arrange the meat portions in it.
6. Pour 1 tbsp of olive oil over the meat.
7. Close the lid of your Ninja Foodi and press the button "Air Crisp" and set the timer to 35 minutes.
8. Set the temperature to about 360° F
9. In the meantime, add the vegetables to the basket of the Ninja Foodi and Air Crisp for 5 minutes
10. Heat the tortillas for a short time in a non stick pan and brush it with the melted butter.
11. Serve your beef meat with the tortillas and enjoy it!

- Use amasai for topping
- Avocado

Nutrition Information

Calories: 481.8| Fat: 21.7g | Carbohydrates: 52.4 g | Fiber: 3.4g |Protein: 20.5g

Recipe 8: Beef Curry

TIME TO PREPARE
10 minutes

COOK TIME
30 Minutes

SERVING
4 People

Ingredients

- 1 Pound of minced beef
- 1 large sliced onion
- 1 Pinch of ginger
- 3 Minced cloves of garlic
- ½ Teaspoon of chilli powder
- ½ Teaspoon of turmeric
- 1 Teaspoon of paprika
- 1 Teaspoon of ground cumin
- 2 Potatoes
- 1 tbsp of tomato puree
- 1 teaspoon of sugar
- ½ Cup of peas
- ½ teaspoon of Garam Masala

Instructions

1. Preheat your Ninja Foodi by pressing the setting button SEAR/SAUTE
2. Sauté the onion in a little bit of oil.
3. Add the minced beef and season it with salt and black pepper.
4. Roll the minced beef into balls and arrange it in the Air Crisp basket
5. Set the heat at 350° F and the timer to 15 minutes using the button "Air Crisp"
6. When the beef balls are cooked, remove it from the Ninja Foodi
7. Place the meatballs in the Pressure cook insert.
8. Add the ginger, the garlic and the red chilli
9. Add in the paprika, the cumin and the turmeric.
10. Keep stirring.
11. Meanwhile, chop the potatoes into tiny cubes.
12. Add the potatoes to the Ninja Foodi .
13. Fry the mixture very well.
14. Add the tomato and the sugar.
15. Add the salt and a little bit of water to the peas.
16. Close the lid of the Ninja Foodi and set the timer to

- Leaves of coriander

15 minutes at High pressure
17. When you are about to turn off your Ninja Foodi; then do a quick release of pressure
18. Open the lid when it is safe to do; then add in the Masala and keep stirring.
19. Finally, garnish your curry with chopped coriander

Nutrition Information

Calories: 266| Fat: 13g | Carbohydrates: 11 g | Fiber: 2.9g |Protein: 29g

Recipe 9: Curried Beef Liver

TIME TO PREPARE
5 minutes

COOK TIME
25 Minutes

SERVING
5 People

Ingredients

- ½ lb of beef liver
- 1 sliced onion
- 1 large tomato
- 1 minced clove of garlic
- 1 teaspoon of ginger
- 1.5 Teaspoon of paprika
- 1/2 Teaspoon of chilli powder
- 1 Teaspoon of cumin powder
- 1/2 Teaspoon of ground coriander
- 1/2 Teaspoon of turmeric
- 1/2 Teaspoon of Garam Masala
- 1/2 Teaspoon of sugar
- A few coriander leaves

Instructions

1. Finely chop the onion
2. Start your Ninja Foodi by pressing the setting function "SEAR/SAUTE"
3. Sauté the onion for about 3 minutes
4. Add in the ginger and the garlic and stir.
5. Now, add your grated ginger and the garlic.
6. Keep stirring.
7. Add your powdered spices; then fry it for 3 minutes.
8. Meanwhile, season the liver with the salt and the pepper
9. Add in the liver and close the lid of the Ninja Foodi
10. Press the button function "PRESSURE COOK"
11. Set the timer to 15 minutes.
12. Set the temperature to 350° F
13. When the cooking time is over, turn off the Ninja Foodi and do a quick pressure release
14. Add the chopped tomato and the sugar and pour a little bit of water; then sauté for about 6 additional minutes
15. Garnish the dish with the coriander.

Nutrition Information

Calories: 329.5| Fat: 8.2g | Carbohydrates: 26.7 g | Fiber: 5.6g |Protein: 32.2g

Recipe 10: Ninja Foodi Lamb with Orange

TIME TO PREPARE
6 minutes

COOK TIME
10 Minutes

SERVING
5 People

Ingredients

- 2 racks of lamb
- 1 tbsp of olive oil
- 1 pinch of salt
- 1 pinch of ground black pepper
- 1 cup of fresh leaves of parsley
- 2 minced garlic cloves.
- 1 orange grated zest
- ¾ cup of toasted and finely chopped pecan nuts
- 2 tablespoons of Dijon mustard

Instructions

1. Preheat your Ninja Foodi by pressing the button "SEAR/SAUTE"
2. Rub the lamb using olive oil
3. Season the lamb with salt, olive oil and pepper.
4. Pour in 2 tablespoons of water; then arrange the lamb in the Ninja Foodi insert
5. Set the timer to 12 minutes and the pressure to High
6. Meanwhile, mix the garlic, the parsley, the orange zest and the pecan nuts all in a deep bowl.
7. When the timer beeps; do a quick pressure release; then remove the racks of lamb of Ninja Foodi
8. Spread on each of lamb rack 1tbsp of Dijon mustard, herbs and nuts.
9. Divide the mixture between the racks of the lamb evenly
10. Place the lamb in the Air Crisp basket of your Ninja Foodi and Air Crisp for about 10 additional minutes.
11. Serve and enjoy your dish with salads!

Nutrition Information

Calories: 283.2| Fat: 8.8g | Carbohydrates: 16.5 g | Fiber: 1.3g |Protein: 32.4g

Recipe 11: Pork with peaches

TIME TO PREPARE
10 minutes

COOK TIME
25 Minutes

SERVING
5 People

Ingredients

- 7 peaches
- ¼ Cup of water
- 3 cups of sugar
- 1 ½ lbs of pork portions
- 4 tbsp of Yazoo's Ultimate roast Rub
- 7 tbsp of brown sugar

Instructions

1. Start by peeling and pitting 7 peaches, and then cut it into cubes.
2. Take a deep pot and pour water into it, then add sugar.
3. Cook the mixture all together for 40 minutes until the mixture thickens.
4. Now, add the food to the process.
5. Puree it.
6. Rub the pork meat with the roasting seasoning, and set it aside for the entire night to marinate.
7. Once you are ready to cook, place the pork meat in your Ninja Foodi
8. Close the lid of your Ninja Foodi and press the button "Pressure Cook"
9. Set the temperature to about 350°F and the timer to 20 minutes; make sure the valve to sealed Position
10. Once your meat is ready and no longer pink, turn off your Ninja Foodi and do a quick pressure release

11. Remove the meat from the Ninja Foodi
12. Mix it with 1tbsp of sugar (For each portion)
13. Cut the peaches in halves and remove the pit, but leave the skin.
14. Mix 1 tbsp of brown sugar with 1 teaspoon of roast to rub each peach.
15. Place back the meat in your Ninja Foodi and press the button "SEAR/SAUTE" and sauté for about 2 minutes.
16. Serve your meat and enjoy an amazing dish.
17. Serve with peach

Nutrition Information

Calories: 333.6| Fat: 14.6g | Carbohydrates: 34.6g | Fiber: 2.4g |Protein: 21.6g

Recipe 112: Pulled Pork

TIME TO PREPARE
10 minutes

COOK TIME
17 Minutes

SERVING
3 People

Ingredients

- 1 lb of Pork Tenderloin
- 1 Tbsp of Olive Oil
- ½ Tbsp of Paprika
- ½ Tbsp of dry Mustard
- 1 tsp of Kosher Salt
- 1 tsp of Black Pepper
- ½ tsp of cumin
- 1 Tbsp of Swerve Brown
- ¾ Cup of low Sodium Chicken Broth
- ¾ Cup of BBQ Sauce, divided
- 2 Tbsp of Hot Sauce

Instructions

1. Mix the salt with the pepper, the paprika, the dry mustard, the cumin, and the brown sugar all together in a small bowl.
2. Combine the chicken broth with about ¼ cup of BBQ sauce, and any type of optional hot sauce in a separate bowl; then set aside.
3. Rub the olive oil over the pork tenderloin; then coat both the sides of the pork with the spices
4. Turn your Foodi SEAR/SAUTE function on the HI setting and once the pot is hot; add in the pork tenderloin with the mixed spices. Then coat both sides of the pork tenderloin with the mixed spices.
5. Turn the Foodi's sauté function on its HI setting and once the pot is hot; add in the pork tenderloin and cook for about 2 minutes
6. Flip the meat and cook for about 2 additional minutes
7. Pour in the broth mixture; then seal the Foodi; then pressure cook on HI for about 10 to 12 minutes at a High pressure

8. Transfer the cooked pork tenderloin to a large bowl
9. Turn on the Foodi by pressing the function button "SEAR/SAUTE" on HI and sauté for about 5 minutes
10. Shred the pork tenderloin with two forks; then pour in the remaining ½ cup of BBQ sauce and stir back to your Ninja Foodi
11. Serve and enjoy your pulled pork

Nutrition Information

Calories: 140| Fat: 4g | Carbohydrates: 8 g | Fiber: 1g |Protein: 17g

Recipe 13: Pork Carnitas

TIME TO PREPARE
7 minutes

COOK TIME
18 Minutes

SERVING
4 People

Ingredients

- 2 lbs of pork butt chopped into pieces of about 2 inch each
- 1 tsp of kosher salt
- ½ tsp of oregano
- ½ tsp of cumin
- 1 Orange, cut into half
- 1 Peeled and cut into half, yellow onion
- 6 Peeled and crushed garlic cloves
- ½ Cup of chicken broth

Instructions

1. Place the pork, the salt, the oregano, and the cumin in your Ninja Foodi pressure cook insert.
2. Combine your ingredients very well and make are the seasonings are covering the meat
3. Take the orange and squeeze the juices over the pork.
4. Place the squeezed orange in the pressure cook insert together with the onion, the garlic cloves and about ½ cup of chicken broth
5. Cover your Ninja Foodi with the pressure cooker lid and make sure the valve is in sealed position
6. Set your Ninja Foodi to High Pressure and cook for about 20 minutes
7. Once the pressure cooking time is complete, do a quick release pressure by switching the valve to vent and once the pressure is fully released; open the lid and remove the orange, the onion and the garlic

cloves

8. Set your Ninja Foodi to SEAR/SAUTE and select the md:hi; and cook for about 10 minutes
9. Press the stop on your Ninja Foodi and close the Air Crisp lid
10. Select the setting function Broil and adjust the time to about 8 minutes
11. Top with parsley; then serve and enjoy your pork Carnitas!

Nutrition Information

Calories: 355| Fat: 13g| Carbohydrates: 27.6 g | Fiber: 1g |Protein: 43g

Recipe 14: Stuffed Pork Chops

TIME TO PREPARE
5 minutes

COOK TIME
15 Minutes

SERVING
4 People

Ingredients

- 1 ½ Thick center cut boneless pork chops, butterflied
- ¼ Cup of shredded mozzarella
- ¼ Cup of sun-dried tomatoes
- 2/3 Cup of spinach
- 2 Sautéd, chopped garlic cloves
- 1 Tablespoon of olive oil
- BBQ rub
- 1 Pinch of black pepper
- Smashed garlic
- Herbs
- 1 Pinch of sea salt
- 1 Pinch of seasoning blend

Instructions

1. Oil and season the pork chop.
2. Start with the pork flat; then add the pork chops as well as your ingredients to the Ninja Foodi
3. Add the chopped garlic, the sun-dried tomatoes, the spinach, and the shredded mozzarella cheese.
4. Fold the pork chops closed and secure with a cooking twine or toothpicks
5. Place the pork chops in your Air Crisp basket with the rack in low position.
6. Air Crisp the pork chops at a temperature of about 390°F for about 15 to 16 minutes
7. Once perfectly cooked; serve and enjoy your dish!

Nutrition Information

Calories: 222.5| Fat: 5.7g | Carbohydrates: 13.5 g | Fiber: 0.5g |Protein: 24.1g

CHAPTER 2: DESSERT, BREAD AND ROLL RECIPES

Recipe 15: Ninja Foodi Chocolate Cake

TIME TO PREPARE
10 minutes

COOK TIME
22 Minutes

SERVING
6-7 People

Ingredients

- 1 ½ cups of Brown Sugar
- 1 Cup of All-purpose Flour
- ½ cup of Unsweetened Cocoa Powder
- ¾ Teaspoon of Baking Powder
- ¾ Teaspoon of Baking Soda
- ½ Teaspoon of Salt
- 1 Large beaten egg
- ½ Cup of Milk
- ¼ Cup of Vegetable Oil
- 1 teaspoon of Vanilla Extract
- ½ Cup of Hot Water

Instructions

1. In a deep and a medium bowl, mix the sugar, the flour, the cocoa powder, the baking powder and the baking soda with salt.
2. Add the eggs, the milk, the oil and the vanilla extract to your mixture.
3. Now, smoothly mix your mixture slowly.
4. Add the small quantity of hot water; after that, stir the mixture evenly.
5. Don't feel that your mixture is ruined when you notice the batter starting to thin. It is perfect.
6. Now, pour your mixture into the pan you are going to use, make sure it fits your Ninja Foodi
7. Place a rack in low position in your Ninja Foodi
8. Pour 1 cup of water in your Ninja Foodi; then cover your cake using a foil, and then poke it gently making a few holes in the cake.
9. Put your tray in the basket of the Ninja Foodi and slide on the rack in your Ninja Foodi and close the lid
10. Set the temperature to 320° F and the pressure to High for about 20 to 22 minutes using the

button BAKE/ROAST
11. Once the timer beeps, do a quick release pressure for about 10 minutes; then open the lid when it is safe to do it and remove the foil from your cake
12. Make sure to let the cake rest for 10 minutes before removing it from the tray.
13. Serve and enjoy your cake when it cools down!

Nutrition Information

Calories: 249| Fat: 12.8g | Carbohydrates: 1g | Fiber: 1.4g |Protein: 2.2g

Recipe 16: Apple Cobbler

TIME TO PREPARE
5 minutes

COOK TIME
25 Minutes

SERVING
4 People

Ingredients

- 1 Can of about 21 ounces of apple fruit filling
- 1 Package of about 15 ounces yellow cake mix 1/2 Cup butter cut into thin slices

Instructions

1. Spray a 9 inches Pie Tin with a Non-stick cooking spray
2. Spread the apple pie filling inyo the bottom of the tin
3. Top with about ¾ of the dry cake mixture; then top with the butter in one layer; try to cover all the areas of the cake mixture; don't leave any exposed
4. Place the pie tin in a cooking pot with a sling place underneath it
5. Close the lid; then select the button "BAKE/ROAST"
6. Set the temperature to about 350°F and the timer to about 25 minutes
7. Select the button "start"; then open the crisping lid 5 minutes after the cooking time starts
8. Place a piece to cover; then close the crisping lid.
9. Check after about 20 minutes; then tests with a toothpick

10. Scoop out with a spoon; then serve and enjoy cold with ice cream!
11. Make sure the top is not browning too much.
12. Test with toothpick at 25 minutes. It should come out clean.
13. Scoop out with a big spoon. Serve it warm or cold. With ice cream or without.

Nutrition Information

Calories: 351| Fat: 14g | Carbohydrates: 57g | Fiber: 3g |Protein: 2g

Recipe 17: Banana Cinnamon cake

TIME TO PREPARE
5 minutes

COOK TIME
7 Minutes

SERVING
3 People

Ingredients

- 1 Cup of butter
- 1/3 Cup of brown sugar
- 1 large beaten egg
- 1 Mashed banana
- 2 tbsp of honey
- 1 Cup of flour
- ½ Teaspoon of cinnamon
- 1 Pinch of salt

Instructions

1. Prepare a ring tin tray to bake the cake in
2. In a deep bowl, beat your butter together with the sugar until it becomes creamy.
3. Add the beaten egg, the banana and the honey
4. Whisk the egg into the mixture of the butter until it becomes smooth.
5. Add the flour, the cinnamon and the salt.
6. Mix the batter very well.
7. Transfer your batter to the ring tin; then use the back of your spoon in order to evenly level its surface.
8. Now, place a rack in a low position in your Ninja Foodi and pour in 1 cup of water; then place the cake over the rack and cover with a foil in the Ninja Foodi; then cover with the lid
9. Set the timer to about 25 minutes and the temperature to 320°F
10. Don't remove the cake from the Ninja Foodi until you test it with a toothpick and nothing comes out.
11. When you remove your cake from your Ninja Foodi, let it rest for 10 minutes before serving.
12. Enjoy a delicious cake with coffee or tea!

Nutrition Information

Calories: 270| Fat: 14g | Carbohydrates: 36g | Fiber: 0.5g |Protein: 2g

Recipe 18: Chocolate Cupcakes

TIME TO PREPARE
10 minutes

COOK TIME
20 Minutes

SERVING
6 People

Ingredients

- 1 ½ cups of all purpose flour
- ½ Cup of cocoa powder
- 6 large egg whites
- 1 teaspoon of cream of tartar
- 1 ½ cups of caster sugar
- 1 teaspoon of vanilla extract
- 3 Tablespoons of warm Butter
- 1 cup of sifted icing sugar
- ½ Cup of glace cherries
- Use silver dragees for garnishing

Instructions

1. Sift the flour and the cocoa in a deep bowl.
2. Place the egg whites in the electric processor
3. Add 2tbsp of caster sugar
4. Keep stirring and beating the mixture until you obtain a smooth batter.
5. Fold in the remaining sugar
6. Add the vanilla extract, the flour and the powder of cocoa
7. Grease your baking pan very well using the butter
8. Divide the mixture you have between the small tin cups
9. Pour 1 cup of water in your Ninja Foodi and place a rack in a low position in your Ninja Foodi
10. Place the tin cups on the rack and cover with aluminium foil; then close the lid and bake for about 20 minutes

11. Set the temperature to about 320° F using the button "BAKE/ROAST" and when it is perfectly cooked remove the cup cakes from the Ninja air fryer and set it aside for 5 minutes.
12. Place the icing sugar in a deep bowl, then add a little bit of warm water
13. Add 1 tbsp of until you obtain a smooth icing
14. Top the surface of your cakes with your prepared icing.
15. Quarter your cherries and use it to top and decorate your cakes along with your dragees
16. Serve and enjoy your cup cakes!

Nutrition Information

Calories: 432| Fat: 20g | Carbohydrates: 53g | Fiber: 0g |Protein: 2g

Recipe 19: Cherry and Chocolate Frosted Cake

TIME TO PREPARE
10 minutes

COOK TIME
22 Minutes

SERVING
5 People

Ingredients

- 1 box of chocolate fudge cake
- ¼ lb of cherry pie filling
- 1 teaspoon of almond extract
- 2 large eggs

For the Frosting:

- 1 cup of white sugar
- 5 tbsp of butter
- 1/3 Cup of milk
- 1 Cup of Chocolate Chips

Instructions

1. Mix all together, the cake mixture the filling of the pie, the extract and the eggs in a large bowl
2. Mix very well using your hand, then spread the mixture above a jelly pan of roll shape
3. Pour 1cup of water in your Ninja Foodi; then place a trivet or rack in a low position
4. Place the pan on the rack and cover with aluminum Foil
5. Close the lid of the Ninja Foodi and press the button "Pressure Cook" and bake for about 20 minutes at High pressure
6. For frosting the cake, combine the sugar, the butter and the milk, then stir on a considerably low heat.
7. Boil the mixture for 2 minutes.
8. Add the chocolate chips for a few seconds
9. When the timer of the Ninja Foodi beeps; turn it off; then do a quick release pressure

10. Decorate your cake with the prepared frost
11. Serve your cake and enjoy it!

Nutrition Information

Calories: 309.8| Fat: 13.6g | Carbohydrates: 43.4g | Fiber: 0.8g |Protein: 3.8g

Recipe 20: Chocolate Cheesecake

TIME TO PREPARE
8 minutes

COOK TIME
15 Minutes

SERVING
4 People

Ingredients

- The crust of Chocolate cookies
- Crushed chocolate cookie crumbs
- 3 Tbsp of melted butter
- Triple filling for the chocolate
- 1 Cup of cream cheese
- 2/3 Cup of sugar
- 5 Medium eggs
- ½ Cup of sour cream
- ½ Cup of whipping cream
- 1/3 Cup of liqueur, cream of cacao
- 1 and ¼ teaspoons of vanilla extract
- 1 cup of chocolate
- 1 cup of German and

Instructions

1. For the crust: In a deep small bowl, stir all together the crushed cookies and the melted butter until the ingredients become very well combined.
2. Press the mixture of the crumb on the bottom of a spring form pan.
3. Now for the filling: In a medium bowl, combine the cream cheese and the sugar.
4. Beat the ingredients using a mixer until the ingredients become smooth.
5. Add the eggs, one by one and make sure to beat very well after each addition of the eggs.
6. Stir in the sour cream while continuously whipping the cream, the crème de cacao, and the vanilla extract.
7. Stir in the melted semisweet chocolate and the grated German chocolate.
8. Pour the mixture of cheese cream above the crust.
9. Pour 1 cup of water in your Ninja Foodi; then place a rack in a low position

grated sweet chocolate

10. Place the pan with the pie in it and cover with an aluminum Foil
11. Close the lid of the Ninja Foodi and set the temperature to about 350°F for about 15 minutes at High pressure
12. When the timer beeps; do a quick release pressure; then open the lid when it is safe to do and set the cake aside for about 10 minutes
13. Serve your cake with the cocoa powder dusted on top and enjoy!

Nutrition Information

Calories: 257| Fat: 18g | Carbohydrates: 20.5g | Fiber: 0.3g |Protein: 4.4g

Recipe 21: Chocolate Fondant

TIME TO PREPARE
5 minutes

COOK TIME
12 Minutes

SERVING
2-3 People

Ingredients

- 2Tbsp of self Raising Flour
- 4Tbsp of Caster Sugar
- 2 cups of Dark Chocolate
- 2 cups of Butter
- 1 Orange (to use its rind and juice)
- 2 Large Eggs

Instructions

1. Grease a number of 4 ramekins with cooking spray
2. Melt the chocolate with the butter in a deep glass dish and over a large pan of warm water.
3. Stir your ingredients until you obtain a very nice and creamy texture.
4. Whisk, and then beat your eggs and the sugar until they become frothy.
5. Now, add the orange together with the mixture of egg and the mixture of sugar into the chocolate.
6. Now, add the quantity of flour and mix everything evenly.
7. Fill your ramekins until they are approximately 75% full.
8. Pour 1 cup of water in your Ninja Foodi and place a rack in it; then put the ramekins on the rack and cover with a foil

9. Close the lid of the Ninja Foodi and press "Pressure cook"; then set your timer to 12 minutes at High pressure; make sure the vakve is in Sealed position
10. When the pressure cooking time ends; do a quick release pressure; then open the lid when it is safe to do it
11. Flip the ramekins upside down on the serving plate
12. Carefully, tap using a knife to release the fondant from the bottom centre the bottom with a blunt knife as this will loosen the edges.
13. Serve your fondant with the vanilla and the ice cream or the caramel sauce.
14. Enjoy your dessert!

Nutrition Information

Calories: 179.3| Fat: 3g | Carbohydrates: 22.5g | Fiber: 3.3g |Protein: 16.6g

Recipe 22: Orange and cherry cake

TIME TO PREPARE
10 minutes

COOK TIME
20 Minutes

SERVING
4 People

Ingredients

- 2 Cups of Self Raising Flour
- ½ Cup of Butter
- ¾ Cup of Sugar
- 2 Large separated eggs
- ½ Cup of Desiccated Coconut
- ¾ Glace of sliced Cherries
- 1 Cup of Orange juice

Instructions

1. Start by greasing a loaf pan and keep it aside.
2. Now beat the butter with the use of an electric mixer
3. Add the sugar and beat it very well until it becomes light and a little bit fluffy.
4. Add the yolks and keep beating until the mixture is perfectly combined.
5. Stir in the coconut and the cherries.
6. Now, add the sifted flour together with the half of the orange juice.
7. Add what was left of the flour
8. Stir in the orange juice
9. In a bowl, beat the egg whites until you notice the mixture becomes smooth.

10. Pour 1 cup of water in the Ninja Foodi; then place a rack at a low position in it
11. Place the cake pan on the rack or trivet and cover with a foil
12. Press the button Pressure Cook and bake your cake at a High pressure for about 20 minutes
13. When the timer beeps; do a quick releas pressure; then open the lid when it is safe to do it
14. Remove the cake from the Ninja Foodi; then set it aside to cool at least, for 10 minutes.
15. Serve and enjoy your cake!

Nutrition Information

Calories: 195| Fat: 10.3g | Carbohydrates: 23g | Fiber: 0g |Protein: 2.4g

Recipe 23: Homemade Bread

TIME TO PREPARE
10 minutes

COOK TIME
30 Minutes

SERVING
3-4 People

Ingredients

- 3 Cups of flour all-purpose flour plus extra for flouring surface
- 1 Cup of water warmed to about 105° F.
- 1 Teaspoon of sea salt
- 2 Teaspoons of White Sugar
- 2 and ¼ teaspoons of active instant or dry yeast
- 1 tbsp of olive oil

Instructions

1. Place one tablespoon of warm water in a small cup or bowl
2. Stir and let the cup sit aside until you see bubbles coming out of the yeast, the whole process can take no more than 5 minutes.
3. Combine about 3 cups of flour with salt in a medium mixing bowl
4. Add the bloomed mixture of yeast; then stir very well
5. Slowly add the warm water and stir as you go; then turn the dough onto a floured surface and start kneading; making sure to bring in the loose flour in each turn
6. Knead for about 15 minutes; then add in 1 tablespoon of olive oil to the inner pot of your Ninja Foodi
7. Coat the top of your dough ball with oil; then cover with a damp towel and set the dehydration mode to a temperature of about 105°F for about 30 minutes
8. Remove the dough; then punch it down and reform it into the shape of bread, whether round or square to your liking; then return it to your Ninja Foodi's

inner pot and cover with a damp towel and set the dehydration mode to a temperature of about 105° F for about 30 minutes.
9. Remove the towel of the dough; then score the top of the dough loaf with a knife in three lines
10. Set the function "Bake" to about 325°F and bake for about 30 minutes just an hour before cutting it
11. Slice the bread; then serve and enjoy your dish!
12. Bake function to 325° F and bake for 30 minutes.

Nutrition Information

Calories: 129| Fat: 1g | Carbohydrates: 24g | Fiber: 1g |Protein: 3g

Recipe 24: Sourdough Bread

TIME TO PREPARE
20 minutes

COOK TIME
40 Minutes

SERVING
5 People

Ingredients

- 1 and ½ cups of water, divided
- 1 and ½ teaspoons of instant or of active dry yeast
- 1 teaspoon of sugar
- 3 Cups of all-purpose flour
- 1 Cup of plain Greek yogurt
- 2 Teaspoons of kosher salt

Instructions

1. Warm about ½ cup of water to a 110° F; then combine with the yeast and the sugar in the bowl of a mixer and let sit until the mixture becomes foamy, about 4 to 5 minutes.
2. Add the flour, the yogurt, and the salt to the yeast mixture and attach the bowl to a stand mixer fitted with a dough hook attachment.
3. Mix on a medium-low speed for about 2 minutes.
4. Scrape down the sides of a bowl with a rubber spatula; then increase the speed to a medium speed for about 5 minutes.
5. Warm your Ninja Foodi by pressing the setting function 250°F and to about 1 minute
6. Select the button START/STOP to begin; then shape the dough into a smooth ball and place it in the preheated pot; then cover with a kitchen towel and let the dough rest for about 2 hours
7. In the meantime; cut a round parchment paper that fits the reversible rack; then place it on the rack in the Ninja Foodi in low position and grease with

cooking spray

8. Once the dough has perfectly risen; transfer it to a lightly floured surface; then shape it into a ball and cover with a kitchen towel and let rest for about 15 minutes
9. Make a deep line in the dough using a very sharp knife right into the center
10. Pour the remaining 1 cup of water in the pot; then place the rack with the dough in the Ninja Foodi inner pot and close the crisping lid.
11. Select the function button "ROAST" and set the temperature to about 325° F and the timer to about 40 minutes
12. Select the START/STOP to start cooking; then when the cooking time is complete; remove your loaf from the Ninja Foodi and set over a cooling rack for about 2 hours
13. Serve and enjoy your dish!

Nutrition Information

Calories: 100| Fat: 1g | Carbohydrates: 20g | Fiber: 4g |Protein: 6g

Recipe 25: Flat bread with cheese

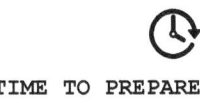

TIME TO PREPARE
10 minutes

COOK TIME
8 Minutes

SERVING
6-7 People

Ingredients

- 1 Tube of commercially prepared pizza dough
- ½ cup of butter
- 1 tsp of garlic
- 1 Sprinkle of fresh or dried parsley
- 1 Pinch of dried Italian seasoning
- 2 Cups of shredded Mozzarella cheese
- Other preferred toppings of your choice

Instructions

1. Open the pizza dough and unroll it; then check for any holes or cracks
2. Reroll your dough on the long side; then cut into rolls of 1" each; then flatter each to about 6" of diameter
3. Combine the butter with the garlic, and the herbs; then brush over the top of your dough
4. Place the rolls into your Ninja Foodi rack
5. Air crisp the dough for about 4 minutes
6. Flip; then brush the dough again with butter and Air Crisp for about 4 additional minutes
7. Sprinkle some cheese over the top of the bread and air fry until the cheese melts
8. Add any toppings of your choice; then serve and enjoy your bread!

Nutrition Information

Calories: 182| Fat: 17g | Carbohydrates: 2g | Fiber: 0g |Protein: 6g

Recipe 26: Pumpkin Bread

TIME TO PREPARE
12 minutes

COOK TIME
40 Minutes

SERVING
4 People

Ingredients

- ½ Cup of pumpkin Puree
- 2 Large eggs
- 1/3 Cup of Vegetable Oil
- ¼ Cup of water
- 1 Cup of Sugar
- 1 and 1/3 cups of All-Purpose Flour
- ¾ Teaspoon of Baking Soda
- ¼ Teaspoon of salt
- 1/3 Teaspoon of ground Cinnamon
- 1 Teaspoon of Pumpkin Pie Spice
- Powdered Sugar

Instructions

1. Combine the pumpkin, the eggs, the oil, and the water in a large mixing bowl or in a stand mixer.
2. Mix your ingredients very well; then add in the sugar, the flour, the baking soda, the salt, the cinnamon and the pumpkin pie spice.
3. Mix your ingredients until the dough is formed.
4. Place the dough in a greased pan; pan or loaf pan.
5. Place the pan with the dough on the prepared wire rack and make sure it is ready to get into your Ninja Foodi on the wire rack
6. Make sure to place the wire rack in your Ninja Foodi in a low position with the handles up
7. Close the lid of your Ninja Foodi and press the button "Bake"; then set the timer to 40 minutes and the temperature to 325°F
8. Remove the pumpkin bread from the Ninja Foodi; then let cool and serve
9. You can sprinkle powdered sugar on top of the bread
10. Serve and enjoy!

Nutrition Information

Calories: 261| Fat: 7 Carbohydrates: 46g | Fiber: 1g |Protein: 4g

Recipe 27: Non Knead Bread

TIME TO PREPARE
10 minutes

COOK TIME
35 Minutes

SERVING
3-4 People

Ingredients

- 3 Cups of bread flour
- 1 Teaspoon of kosher salt
- 1/3 Cup of Baking Cranberries
- ¼ Cup of finely diced pecan
- 1 and ½ cups of lukewarm water
- 1 and ½ teaspoons of active dry yeast
- 1 Tablespoon of honey

Instructions

1. Mix the lukewarm with the water and honey; then stir very well to combine.
2. Add in the yeast and cover; then wait for about 10 minutes
3. Combine the flour with the salt, the cranberries and the pecan in a bowl and set it aside
4. Pour the yeast water into the bowl of the flour and fold until the flour is completely incorporated
5. Place the bread dough in a greased Ninja Foodi and cover with a clean towel; then press the button "Dehydrate" and set for about 4 hours
6. When the time is up; sprinkle a working surface with a little bit of flour
7. Transfer the dough to the working surface from your Ninja Foodi
8. Roll the dough into the shape of a ball without overworking it; then tuck any extra dough onto the bottom side.
9. Let the dough rest for about 15 minutes
10. Place a rack in a low position in your Ninja Foodi; then grease a loaf pan with cooking spray and spread the dough in it

11. Place the pan over the trivet in your Ninja Foodi and press the button "BAKE" and bake for about 35 to 40 minutes
12. Remove the lid and transfer to a cooling rack and set to cool for about 20 minutes
13. Serve and enjoy your bread!

Nutrition Information

Calories: 114| Fat: 0.3 | Carbohydrates: 23.8g | Fiber: 0.8g |Protein: 3.2g

Recipe 28: Zucchini Bread

TIME TO PREPARE
10 minutes

COOK TIME
40 Minutes

SERVING
5 People

Ingredients

- 2 large eggs
- ¾ Cup of sugar
- 1 Teaspoon of vanilla
- ⅓ cup of vegetable oil or canola
- 1 and ½ cups of grated zucchini
- ½ Teaspoon of sea salt, fine grind
- ¾ tsp of cloves ground
- ½ Tbsp of ground cinnamon
- 1 Cup of flour
- 2 Teaspoons of baking powder

Instructions

1. Butter and flour a loaf pan
2. Preheat your Ninja Foodi on about 275° F for about 10 minutes.
3. Grate the zucchini with the help of a box grater
4. Mix 2 eggs with ¾ cup of sugar, 1 tsp of vanilla, and ⅓ cup of vegetable oil in a medium mixing bowl and whisk together
5. Add in the cinnamon, the cloves, the salt, the flour, and the baking powder to your wet ingredients and stir very well to combine
6. Add in the grated zucchini and pour the batter into the loaf pan
7. Set the pan over the rack in a low position in the inner pot of your Ninja Foodi; then press the button Bake/Roast to about 275° F and bake for about 35 to 40 minutes
8. Remove the bread to cool on a baking rack for about 30 to 60 minutes
9. Serve and enjoy your bread!

Nutrition Information

Calories: 157| Fat: 7g | Carbohydrates: 22g | Fiber: 1g |Protein: 2g

Recipe 29: Soda Bread

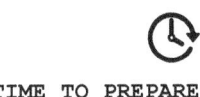
TIME TO PREPARE
8 minutes

COOK TIME
40 Minutes

SERVING
6 People

Ingredients

- 2 Cups of buttermilk
- 1 Cup of golden raisins
- 4 Cups of flour plus extra if needed
- 2 Teaspoons of baking powder
- 2 tsp of baking soda
- 1 tsp of sea salt, fine grind
- 1 Teaspoon of caraway seeds
- ½ Cup of brown sugar
- 1 and ¼ tsp of ground cinnamon
- 1 tsp of vanilla extract

Instructions

1. Soak the Raisins into buttermilk for about 15 to 20 minutes.
2. Preheat your Ninja Foodi to a temperature of about 350° F.
3. Combine your dry ingredients and mix very well together.
4. Add the buttermilk, the raisins, and the vanilla extract; then mix with a large scraper
5. Mix all together very well until it your get a loose dough
6. Dust a pastry mat and dump the dough over a floured surface
7. Knead the dough for about 6 to 7 minutes; then add a little quantity of flour if the dough is sticking
8. Shape the dough in a round flat disc shape, of about the size of the inner pot of your Ninja Foodi.
9. Add 1 tablespoon of butter to the inner pot of your Ninja Foodi; then let melt and move the butter around
10. Cut the shape of X onto the top of your bread
11. Place the bread in the inner pot of your Ninja Foodi
12. Decrease the temperature for about 330° F and bake for about 40 minutes.
13. When the time is up, flip your bread; then let sit in

your Ninja Foodi with the Tender Crisp lid down; then make sure the Ninja Foodi is turned off and let sit for about 20 minutes in your Ninja Foodi
14. Make sure the Ninja Foodi is turned off and let sit in your Foodi for about 20 minutes. This
15. Remove your bread from the Ninja Foodie and let cool for 30 to 60 minutes
16. Serve and enjoy your bread!

Nutrition Information

Calories: 149| Fat: 2.4g | Carbohydrates: 31g | Fiber: 1g |Protein: 3g

Recipe 30: Cashew Bread

TIME TO PREPARE
7 minutes

COOK TIME
40 Minutes

SERVING
5 People

Ingredients

- 2Tbsp of vegetable oil to grease your loaf pan
- 2 and ½ cups of whole raw cashews
- 7 Tbsp of coconut flour
- 8 Beaten large eggs
- ½ Cup of milk
- 4 Teaspoons of apple cider vinegar
- 4 teaspoons of baking powder
- 1 Teaspoon of salt

Instructions

1. Preheat your Ninja Foodi it to about 325° F
2. Grease a loaf pan that fits your Ninja Foodi
3. Set your dish aside and in the mean time; combine the coconut flour, the cashews, the eggs, the milk, the apple cider vinegar, the salt and the baking powder and process the mixture for around 30 to 40 seconds
4. Once the mixture becomes very thick, add 1 to 2 tbsp of water and process again until the mixture becomes smooth
5. Transfer your batter to your already prepared loaf pan
6. Place a rack in a low position in your Ninja Foodi
7. Place the loaf pan onto the racket in your Ninja Foodi and cover with the lid
8. Press the button BAKE/ROAST and bake for t about 40 minutes
9. Once the bread gets a brown color, remove it from the oven and discard it from the parchment paper.
10. Remove the bread from the Ninja Foodi and let cool for 15 minutes
11. Slice the bread; then serve and enjoy it!

Nutrition Information

Calories: 268.8| Fat: 18.9g | Carbohydrates: 21g | Fiber: 2.5g |Protein: 7.3g

Recipe 31: Nuts Bread

TIME TO PREPARE
8 minutes

COOK TIME
20 Minutes

SERVING
5 People

Ingredients

- 1 Cup of all purpose or almond flour
- ¼ Cup of sesame seeds
- ½ Cup of golden flaxseed meal
- ½ Cup of pumpkin seeds
- 1 Cup of sunflower seeds
- 2 Tbsp of chia seeds
- ¼ Cup of water
- 1 and ¼ teaspoon of salt
- 5 Beaten eggs
- 2 Tbsp of sesame seeds to sprinkle it on the top of batter

Instructions

1. Preheat your Ninja Foodi to about 350° F and grease a loaf pan with oil; then line a parchment paper in the loaf pan.
2. In a deep and large bowl; combine all together the almond meal, the sesame seeds, the flaxseed meal, the pumpkin seeds, the sunflower seeds, and the chia seeds
3. Add the salt and mix very well.
4. Pour in the water and the eggs all at once, and stir your ingredients very well until you obtain a smooth batter
5. Pour your batter into the already prepared loaf pan and then sprinkle a pinch of sesame seeds on top of your bread
6. Place a trivet in a low position in your Ninja foodi
7. Press the button "Roast/Bake" and bake your bread for about 40 minutes
8. Remove the bread from your Ninja foodi to a cooling rack and let cool for about 20 minutes
9. Slice the bread into pieces, then serve and enjoy it!

Nutrition Information

Calories: 115.9| Fat: 3.4g | Carbohydrates: 19g | Fiber: 2.4g |Protein: 3.6g

Recipe 32: Dates Bread

TIME TO PREPARE
6 minutes

COOK TIME
40 Minutes

SERVING
4-5People

Ingredients

- 1 Cup of all purpose flour
- ¼ Cup of sesame seeds
- ½ Cup of golden flaxseed meal
- ½ Cup of pumpkin seeds
- 1 Cup of sunflower seeds
- 2 Tbsp of chia seeds
- ¼ Cup of water
- 1 and ¼ teaspoon of salt
- 5 Beaten eggs
- 2 Tbsp of sesame seeds to sprinkle it on the top of batter

Instructions

1. Preheat your Ninja Foodi to about 350° F and grease a loaf pan with oil; then line a parchment paper in the loaf pan.
2. In a deep and large bowl; combine all together the almond meal, the sesame seeds, the flaxseed meal, the pumpkin seeds, the sunflower seeds, and the chia seeds
3. Add the salt and mix very well.
4. Pour in the water and the eggs all at once, and stir your ingredients very well until you obtain a smooth batter
5. Pour your batter into the already prepared loaf pan and then sprinkle a pinch of sesame seeds on top of your bread
6. Place a rack in a low position in your Ninja Foodi
7. Place the baking with the bread Bake the bread for about 40 minutes
8. Remove the bread from the Ninja Foodi and discard it from the parchment paper; then let cool for about 20 minutes
9. Slice the bread into pieces, then serve and enjoy it!

Nutrition Information

Calories: 167.5| Fat: 5.9g | Carbohydrates: 27.9g | Fiber: 1.4g |Protein: 2.8g

Recipe 33: Focaccia Bread

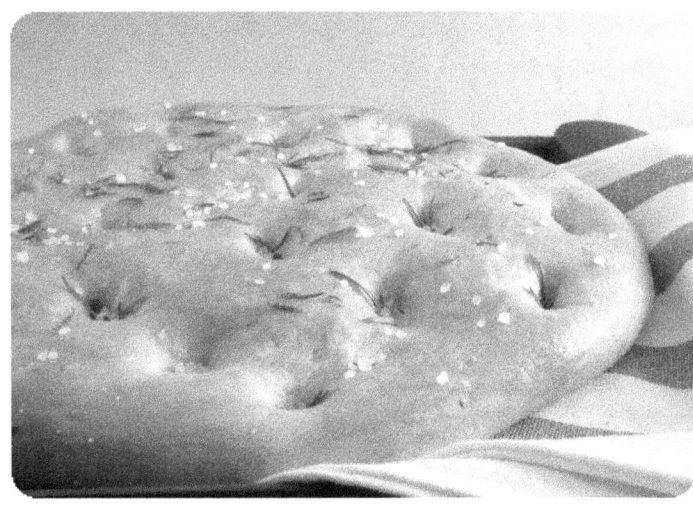

TIME TO PREPARE
8 minutes

COOK TIME
10 Minutes

SERVING
5 People

Ingredients

- 1 Cup of all purpose flour
- 5 tbsp of Psyllium husk
- 2 teaspoon of baking powder
- 1 Teaspoon of salt
- 4 Beaten eggs
- 1 Cup of boiling water

Instructions

1. Preheat your Ninja Foodi to a temperature of 360°F by pressing the button "Bake"
2. In a large and deep mixing bowl, place the psyllium husk with the coconut flour, the baking powder and the salt and stir very well until your ingredients are very well combined.
3. Add the beaten eggs and whisk. Your batter will be very hard and consistent so add 1 cup of boiling water to smooth it.
4. Form your batter into the shape of a Focaccia and place it in a baking tray that is lined with parchment paper.
5. With a sharp knife, cut the diagonally and sprinkle with rosemary, salt and olives.
6. Place a rack in a low position of your Ninja Foodi and
7. Place the baking tray on the rack and bake for about 30 minutes using the button "BAKE/ROAST"
8. When the bread is ready, remove the pan from the and discard the parchment paper
9. Let the bread cool for about 15 minutes
10. Serve your bread warm with butter or cold with

avocado slices and with cheese.

Nutrition Information

Calories: 160| Fat: 3g | Carbohydrates: 29g | Fiber: 1g |Protein: 5g

Recipe 34: Carrot and Orange Bread

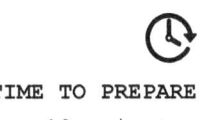

TIME TO PREPARE
10 minutes

COOK TIME
35 Minutes

SERVING
5 People

Ingredients

- 2 Cups of all purpose flour
- 5 Tbsp of coconut flour
- ¼ Cup of granulated stevia
- 1 Teaspoon of cinnamon
- 1 and ½ teaspoons of baking soda
- ¼ Teaspoon of fine sea salt
- 2 large beaten eggs
- 1 Cup of orange juice
- 2 Tbsp of orange zest
- 1 Cup of shredded carrots

Instructions

1. Preheat your Ninja Foodi to about 350°F; then lightly grease a medium loaf pan; then set it aside.
2. In a deep mixing bowl, whisk all together the coconut flour, the almond flour, the sweetener, the cinnamon and the baking soda and the salt; then set the batter aside.
3. In another mixing bowl, whisk the eggs, the orange juice and the zest.
4. Add your dry mixture to the wet batter and whish very well
5. Place a rack in your Ninja Foodi in a low position; then pour the batter into the greased pan and bake it for about 35 minutes
6. Remove the loaf pan and transfer to a cooling rack; then slice the bread
7. Serve and enjoy your bread!

Nutrition Information

Calories: 325| Fat: 16g | Carbohydrates: 42.5g | Fiber: 2.1g |Protein: 2

Recipe 35: Ninja Foodi No Yeast Bread

TIME TO PREPARE
7 minutes

COOK TIME
40 Minutes

SERVING
4 People

Ingredients

- 1 Medium mashed Russet potato, about 1 cup
- 4 Cups of flour; divided
- 4 tsp of baking powder
- ½ tsp of sea salt
- 1 large egg
- 1 Tbsp of olive oil
- 1 cup of Whole Milk
- 1 tsp of butter

Instructions

1. Peel the russet potato and dice it into about ½ to 1 inch the piece
2. Add 2 cups of water with the diced potatoes to the inner pot or your Ninja Foodi
3. Place the pressure lid on your Ninja Foodi and turn the valve to sealed position
4. Pressure cook for about 2 minutes on High; then immediately release the pressure and drain the potatoes
5. Mash the potatoes with a fork; then make sure to get any lumps mashed up
6. Set your ingredients aside to cool; then combine about 3 cups of flour with salt, baking powder and mashed potatoes and mix very well
7. Make a small well; then add in a lightly beaten egg; the milk and the oil
8. Stir your ingredients to combine; you can add an additional ¼ cup of flour
9. Add in 1 cup of flour at a time; then place on a floured surface
10. Preheat your Ninja Foodi on the setting function BAKE/ROAST at a temperature of about 375°F for

about 5 to 10 minutes
11. Knead the dough; then add flour and form a log of it; then place it in a loaf pan
12. Gently press down into a loaf pan and make deep slits into the bread of about 2 inches of depth with a knife
13. Place the loaf pan on a rack in a low position in your Ninja Foodi; then select the button "Bake/ROAST" at a temperature of about 325°F for 30 minutes
14. Remove the cover of your Ninja Foodi and cook for about 20 minutes
15. Brush the top with some butter on top of the bread and loose the tendercrisp lid
16. Flip the bread to a cooling rack; then slice and serve your dish!

Nutrition Information

Calories: 147| Fat: 2g | Carbohydrates: 27g | Fiber: 1g |Protein: 4g

Recipe 36: Wonton Rolls

TIME TO PREPARE
6 minutes

COOK TIME
10 Minutes

SERVING
6 People

Ingredients

- Egg Roll Wrappers
- Egg Roll In a Bowl
- 1 Large egg
- 1 tbsp of water
- Olive oil

Instructions

1. Preheat your Ninja Foodi to 390°F for about 5 minutes
2. Whisk the egg and the water together
3. Place the Egg Roll Mixture in the prepared wrapper.
4. Seal the edges with the egg mixture
5. Spray the egg rolls with a little bit of olive oil
6. Place the egg roll wrappers in your Ninja Foodi Air Crisp basket and bake for about 10 minutes
7. Serve and enjoy your dish!

Nutrition Information

Calories: 142| Fat: 7g | Carbohydrates: 14g | Fiber: 1g |Protein: 5g

Recipe 37: Chicken Wontons

TIME TO PREPARE
5 minutes

COOK TIME
20 Minutes

SERVING
6 People

Ingredients

- 10 Egg Roll Wrappers
- 2 Chicken breasts of about 6 oz Chicken
- 1 Cup of blue Cheese Crumbles
- ¼ Chopped Onion
- A buffalo Sauce
- 1 Packet of Ranch
- 1 Egg

Instructions

1. Place the Frozen chicken in your Ninja Foodi; then pour in 1 cup of chicken broth
2. Pressure cook for about 10 minutes on high pressure
3. Do a quick pressure method for about 5 minutes
4. Once the chicken is perfectly cooked, mix the buffalo sauce with the chopped onion, the ranch packet; the shredded chicken and the bleu cheese crumbles
5. Place the egg rolls wrapper on top of clean surface; then add 3 tablespoons of the mixture to each of the egg rolls.
6. Wrap the corner that is facing you around the filling and roll the egg rolls to form a cylinder; you can use egg wash or water to seal the corners in
7. Air Crisp your egg rolls at a temperature of 375°F for about 8 to 10 minutes in your Ninja Foodi in batches
8. Serve and enjoy with your delicious wontons with your favourite sauce and blue cheese!

Nutrition Information

Calories: 253.9| Fat: 4.1g | Carbohydrates: 29.1g | Fiber: 1.6g |Protein: 20.1g

Recipe 38: Cheese Chips

TIME TO PREPARE
6 minutes

COOK TIME
18 Minutes

SERVING
5 People

Ingredients

- 4 Large egg whites to room temperature
- 4 Tablespoons of shredded Cheddar Cheese
- ½ Tablespoon of water
- 1 Teaspoon of seasoning of your choice

Instructions

1. Using the display panel, touch the button "Air Crisp"; then adjust the temperature to 370°F and the time to about 9 minutes; the press the button Air Crisp
2. Spray two muffin pans with non-stick spray.
3. Whisk the egg whites with water; then season very well
4. Spoon enough mixture of egg whites to cover the bottom of the muffin tin
5. Flatten smoothly with the back of a spoon
6. Sprinkle a pinch of cheese on top of the egg mixture.
7. When you see the display indicating "Add Food"; place both the muffin trays in your Ninja Foodi place both muffin trays in, one on each shelf.
8. Air crisp for about 7 to 9 minutes
9. Serve and enjoy your chips!

Nutrition Information

Calories: 207| Fat: 12g | Carbohydrates: 16g | Fiber: 0g |Protein: 9g

CHAPTER 3: SOUP AND STEW RECIPES

Recipe 39: Pumpkin Soup

TIME TO PREPARE
5 minutes

COOK TIME
12 Minutes

SERVING
4 People

Ingredients

- 1 ½ lbs of butternut squash
- 2 sprig sage
- 1 medium sized chopped onion
- 2 cm of fresh ginger
- 1/4 teaspoon of nutmeg
- 4 cups of vegetable oil
- A pinch of salt
- A pinch of black pepper according to the taste
- Half a cup ½ of toasted pumpkin seeds to use later for garnish.

Instructions

1. Preheat your Ninja Foodi by pressing the button "SEAR/SAUTE"
2. Add your ingredients, except for the pumpkin seeds, the nutmeg and the ginger and sauté for about 5 to 6 minutes
3. When the onion starts softening; scoop them aside and add the rest of the components; the ginger, stock and Nutmeg.
4. Seal your Ninja Foodi pressure cook insert and set the time to about 10 minutes; make sure the valve is in sealed position
5. Set the pressure to High and when the time is up, turn off your Ninja Foodi
6. Now, using a mixer, blend the soup and if it is thick, pour ½ of hot water into it then place it back on the fire in an ordinary sauce pan without selling the lid and in no more than 2 minutes, your soup is ready.
7. Garnish with toasted pumpkin seeds or parsley according to your taste.
8. Serve and enjoy your soup

Nutrition Information

Calories: 220| Fat: 7g | Carbohydrates: 34g | Fiber: 7.6g |Protein: 8.4g

Recipe 40: Cream Soup with bacon

TIME TO PREPARE
5 minutes

COOK TIME
10 Minutes

SERVING
3-4 People

Ingredients

- 1.5 teaspoon of coconut oil
- 4 garlic minced cloves
- 2 medium chopped onions
- 3 Large chopped leeks
- 2 tbsp of ground cumin
- 3 cups of bone broth
- 1 can of coconut milk
- A pinch of sea salt
- A pinch of black pepper
- Chopped parsley or crunchy bacon bits to use for garnish

Instructions

1. In the Ninja Foodi Pressure cooker insert; melt the oil at a low heat by pressing the function "SEAR/SAUTE" and sauté the garlic until it becomes golden, but don't over sauté it, it will ruin the soup and in that case, you have to start all over again.
2. Add your onions and the chopped leeks to the instant Cooking Pot until the ingredients you have put are cooked well and become soft (for about 10 minutes)
3. Add the cumin together with the bone broth to your Ninja Foodi
4. Close the Ninja Foodi and seal the valve; then set the timer to about 10 minutes and the pressure to High
5. At the same time, fry your already chopped bacon in a large wok until they become crunchy.
6. Now, do a quick pressure method; then open the lid when it is safe to do it
7. Add the salt and the black pepper
8. Blend the components in a blender

9. Garnish your soup with the crunchy bacon and parsley then serve it and enjoy!

Nutrition Information

Calories: 120| Fat: 7g | Carbohydrates: 10g | Fiber: 6g |Protein: 2g

Recipe 41: Celeriac Soup

TIME TO PREPARE
5 minutes

COOK TIME
7 Minutes

SERVING
3-4 People

Ingredients

- ½ peeled and cut celeriac into dices
- 3 Teaspoons of coconut oil
- 1 large diced onion
- 1 cup of milk
- 3 cups of chicken stock
- 100g of bacon strips
- 190 g of cremini sliced mushrooms
- 2 cloves of garlic
- 2 teaspoons of fresh and finely chopped chives
- A pinch of salt

A pinch of fresh and ground black pepper(optional

Instructions

1. In your Ninja Foodi Pressure cook insert, melt around 2 teaspoons of the coconut oil using the button "SEAR/SAUTE"
2. Add to the oil, the celeriac and sauté the mixture for around 3 minutes.
3. Add the milk and the chicken stock you have already prepared and let it simmer after locking the Instant Cooking pot for 2 minutes.
4. Meanwhile, take the bacon and fry it in a wok or skillet with a little bit of Oil then remove it from the skillet and cut it into tiny strips.
5. Pour the milk with the chicken to the Ninja Foodi
6. Add the cremini mushroom and the garlic cloves; then close the lid and make sure the valve is in sealed position
7. Pressure cook for about 5 minutes; and when the timer beeps; do a quick pressure release; then open the lid when it is safe to do it and puree the soup with a blender or a mixer
8. Serve and enjoy your soup; then garnish with bacon and mushrooms!

Nutrition Information

Calories: 92.2| Fat: 0.9g | Carbohydrates: 18.7g | Fiber: 6.3g |Protein: 5.7g

Recipe 42: Chicken and vegetables Soup

TIME TO PREPARE
6 minutes

COOK TIME
17 Minutes

SERVING
4 People

Ingredients

- 1 ½ lbs of pastured chicken
- 2 carrots of 1 chopped celery stalk
- 1/2 turnip or you can use radish, cut it into 2 cubes
- 1 tbsp of Italian seasoning or you can use dried parsley or rosemary
- 2 entire bay leaves
- 4 Garlic cloves, minced
- 1 large sliced onion
- 1 tbsp of sea salt
- 1 tbsp of black pepper, freshly ground
- Sliced red onion, or you can use chopped scallion for garnish

Instructions

1. In a preheated Ninja Foodi, put the vegetables
2. Add the chicken and then add the herbs too
3. Press the setting function "SEAR/SAUTE" and sauté your ingredients for about 5 minutes
4. Pour in 2 cups of water
5. Lock the lid of the Ninja Foodi and make sure the Valve is in sealed position
6. Set the timer to about 12 minutes and the temperature to about 360°F
7. When the timer beeps; do a quick Release Pressure
8. Open up the lid of the Ninja Foodi when it is safe to do it and take the bones from the meat.
9. Place the meat back into your Ninja Foodi and stir
10. Smash the carrots and cut the celery; then add to the soup
11. Add the salt and the pepper.
12. Before serving your soup, garnish with the sliced onions or with scallions.

Nutrition Information

Calories: 117| Fat: 7.4g | Carbohydrates: 9.3g | Fiber: 0.2g |Protein: 3.4g

Recipe 43: Beef stew

TIME TO PREPARE
10 minutes

COOK TIME
16 Minutes

SERVING
4 People

Ingredients

- 3 tbsp of vegetable oil
- 1chuck roast of boneless cut into pieces each of 1 inch
- 3 medium sliced onions
- 3 cloves of minced garlic
- 2 Campbell's cans
- 1 can of Condensed Beef Soup
- 1 cup of water
- 2 tbsp chilli powder
- 3 Potatoes; cut them into cubes
- 1 can of drained kernel corn
- Cheddar cheese to taste

Instructions

1. Preheat your Ninja Foodi by pressing the button "SEAR/SAUTE"
2. In the pressure cook insert; place the beef, 2 tbsp of oil; then add in the onion and the minced garlic
3. Pour in 1 cup of broth; the water and the Chilli powder as well as the potatoes; then close the lid and set the timer to about 12 minutes and the pressure to High using the button "Pressure cook"
4. Once the timer beeps; turn off your Ninja Foodi; then do a quick release pressure
5. Open the lid when it is safe to do it; then add in the corn and stir using the SEAR/SAUTE function and cook for about 4 minutes
6. Ladle the stew in bowls; then sprinkle with cheese
7. Serve and enjoy your stew!

Nutrition Information

Calories: 302| Fat: 7g | Carbohydrates: 26g | Fiber: 5 g |Protein: 35g

Recipe 44: Pork Stew

TIME TO PREPARE
6 minutes

COOK TIME
15 Minutes

SERVING
4-5 People

Ingredients

- 2 lbs of boneless pork shoulder, diced into pieces each of 2 inches.
- 1 Cup of Campbell's Condensed Onion Soup
- ½ Cup of apple cider
- 3 large sliced apples
- 3 Cups of peeled butternut squash, peeled (Cut it into pieces 2 inches each)
- 2 Peeled and diced parsnips
- ½ Teaspoon of crushed dried thyme leaves
- 2 Tbsp of oil

Instructions

1. Place the pork in your Ninja Foodi
2. Drizzle the pork with oil
3. Press the button "SEAR/SAUTE" and sauté for about 5 minutes
4. Add in the onion soup, the cider, the apples, the squash, the parsnips, and the thyme.
5. Pour in the water and close the lid; make sure the valve is in sealed position; and pressure cook for about 10 minutes at High Pressure
6. When the timer beeps; turn off your Ninja Foodi; then do a quick release of pressure for 5 minutes
7. Open the lid when it is safe to do
8. Serve and enjoy your pork stew!

Nutrition Information

Calories: 247.2| Fat: 6.2g | Carbohydrates: 41.7g | Fiber: 6.5 g |Protein: 7.5g

Recipe 45: Lamb Stew

TIME TO PREPARE
5 minutes

COOK TIME
20 Minutes

SERVING
4 People

Ingredients

- 1 Pound of Lamb meat
- 4 medium diced potatoes
- 2 large carrots
- 2 ½ cups of lamb stock
- ½ tbsp of black pepper
- ½ tbsp of smoked paprika
- 2 to 4 tbsp of Worcestershire sauce
- 1 tbsp of fresh thyme

Instructions

1. In your Ninja Foodi; and add all the dry ingredients
2. Add the sauce and stir very well.
3. Close the Ninja Foodi with a lid and set the timer for about 20 minutes and the pressure to High using the button Pressure cook; make sure the valve is in sealed position
4. When the timer beeps; turn off the Ninja Foodi and set the valve to venting
5. Do a quick pressure release for about 5 minutes
6. Serve your stew and enjoy its delicious taste!

Nutrition Information

Calories: 259| Fat: 19g | Carbohydrates: 0g | Fiber: 0 g |Protein: 22 g

Recipe 46: Tomato soup

TIME TO PREPARE
8 minutes

COOK TIME
20 Minutes

SERVING
3 People

Ingredients

- 10 large sized tomatoes
- 2 tbsp of olive oil
- ½ tbsp of yellow curcuma powder
- 2 and ½ a cup of water
- 1 tbsp of salt
- 1 tbsp of sugar
- ¼ tbsp of fresh and ground black pepper

Instructions

1. Start your Ninja Foodi by pressing the button "SEAR/SAUTE"
2. After cleaning and washing your tomatoes place them in the Ninja Foodi and sauté for about 3 minutes
3. Remove the tomatoes from the Ninja Foodi.
4. Peel the tomatoes of their skin.
5. Place the tomatoes in the Ninja Foodi pressure cooker insert
6. Pour in 1 ½ cups of warm water, salt and a pinch of pepper.
7. Close the lid of the Ninja Foodi and set the valve to sealed position; and set the timer to 15 minutes; set the pressure to High
8. When the timer beeps; turn off the Ninja Foodi, then do a quick release pressure
9. Open the lid of the Ninja Foodi and process your cooked mixture after it cools down in a processor
10. Sauté for about 3 to 4 minutes
11. You can garnish your soup with parsley and cheese.
12. Serve and enjoy your soup!

Nutrition Information

Calories: 157.3| Fat: 1.4g | Carbohydrates: 32.5g | Fiber: 2.9g |Protein: 3.9g

Recipe 47: Artichoke Soup

TIME TO PREPARE
6 minutes

COOK TIME
15 Minutes

SERVING
4 People

Ingredients

- 1 tbsp of olive oil
- 1 tbsp of butter
- ½ tbsp of yellow curcuma powder
- 1 stick of celery, chop it
- 670 g of artichokes, make sure to peel and chop them.
- 5 Cups of vegetable stock/water
- 1 tea spoon of salt
- ¼ tbsp of ground fresh black pepper
- 1 cup of milk

Instructions

1. In your Ninja Foodi, place in it the butter and the oil then add the curcuma and the celery and sauté for about 2 minutes by pressing the button "SEAR/SAUTE".
2. Now add your artichoke and place all the ingredients all together in the Ninja Foodi and pour in the stock; then close the lid and set the timer for about 10 minutes and the pressure to HIGH
3. When the timer beeps; turn off your Ninja Foodi and do a quick release pressure
4. Open the lid when it is safe to do it
5. Process your soup in a mixer or a blender until it becomes smooth.
6. Return the soup to your Ninja Foodi and press the button "SAUTE"; then add in the salt, the black pepper and sauté for 3 minutes.
7. Add in the milk slowly as you keep stirring
8. Serve your soup after it cools down with bread (toasted)

Nutrition Information

Calories: 94.9| Fat: 2.8g | Carbohydrates: 14.9g | Fiber: 3.8 g |Protein: 4g

Recipe 48: Blacked Eye Pea Stew

TIME TO PREPARE
8 minutes

COOK TIME
20 Minutes

SERVING
4-5 People

Ingredients

- 1 Tablespoon of olive oil
- 1 Diced onion
- 1 Diced celery stalk celery
- 2 Diced carrots
- 1 Finely chopped garlic clove
- 1 and 1/2 cups of cubed smoked ham
- 1 Pound of soaked, rinsed and drained dried black eyed peas
- 6 Cups of vegetable stock
- 1 Tablespoon of smoked paprika
- 2 Bay leaves
- 3 Sprigs of fresh

Instructions

1. Spray your Ninja Foodi pressure cooker insert with cooking spray; then add the onion and sauté it with the carrots for about 2 to 3 minutes
2. Add in the garlic and the ham and sauté for about 2 to 3 minutes
3. Add the ham bone; the pre-soaked black eyed peas, the stock, the smoked paprika, the bay leaves and the thyme and stir very well
4. Stir in the collard greens or the kale and the tomatoes and season with 1 pinch of salt and 1 pinch of ground black pepper
5. Cover your Ninja Foodi with a lid and seal the valve; then set the timer to 15 minutes and the pressure to High
6. When the time is up; turn off your Ninja Foodi; then do a quick release pressure and set aside to cool for about 10 minutes
7. set the pressure cooker aside to cool for about 10 minutes

thyme
- 1 Can of 14 oz of fire roasted diced tomatoes
- 2 Cups of roughly packed chopped kale
- 1 Pinch of salt
- 1 Pinch of ground black pepper

8. When the Ninja Foodi is safe to open; remove the lid e and open it
9. Blend your ingredients with a food processor or a blender
10. Ladle the stew into bowls and top it with chopped chives
11. Serve and enjoy your stew!

Nutrition Information

Calories: 198| Fat: 1g | Carbohydrates: 19g | Fiber: 1 g |Protein: 15g

Recipe 49: Potato Soup

TIME TO PREPARE
7 minutes

COOK TIME
15 Minutes

SERVING
4 People

Ingredients

- 4 Chopped bacon slices
- 2 Large diced potatoes
- 3 Large diced celery stalks
- 1 Large diced onion
- 2 Cups of chicken stock
- 1 to 2 bay leaves
- 2 Sprigs of thyme
- 1 Pinch of salt
- 1 Pinch of freshly ground black pepper
- 2 Tablespoons of flour
- 2 Cups of half and half
- Shredded cheddar cheese
- Fresh, chopped chives

Instructions

1. Turn on your Ninja Foodi by pressing the button "SEAR/SAUTE" and brown the bacon in a little bit of olive oil
2. Remove half of the bacon and set it aside
3. Add the rest of the ingredients into your Ninja Foodi and stir
4. Lock the lid of your Ninja Foodi and seal the valve
5. Cook your soup for about 15 minutes on High pressure
6. When the time is up, turn off your Ninja Foodi and quick release the pressure
7. Add the half and half
8. Blend your soup with a food processor or a blender
9. Ladle the soup in serving bowl and garnish with cheddar, bacon and chives
10. Serve and enjoy your soup!

Nutrition Information

Calories: 146| Fat: 4.7g | Carbohydrates: 25.5g | Fiber: 0 g |Protein: 5.5g

Recipe 50: Broccoli Soup

TIME TO PREPARE
7 minutes

COOK TIME
15 Minutes

SERVING
4 People

Ingredients

- 2 Tablespoons of oil
- 1 Tablespoon of onion Powder
- 2 ½ Cups of Chicken Stock
- 1 Large Bunch of Broccoli
- 1/4 Teaspoon of garlic powder
- 1 Cup of shredded Carrots
- 1 Cup of Heavy Cream
- 2 Cups of shredded sharp cheddar cheese
- 1 Teaspoon of salt
  1 Teaspoon of pepper

Instructions

1. Place the oil in the bottom of your Ninja Foodi Pressure cooker insert; then toss in the onion and sauté it for about 2 minutes
2. Add in the broccoli florets, the carrots, the chicken stock, the garlic powder, the onion powder, the salt and the pepper
3. Close the lid of your Ninja Foodi and secure the lid with the valve
4. Set the temperature to about 10 minutes and the pressure to High
5. When the timer beeps, perform a quick pressure release; then add in the cheese and the heavy cream
6. Transfer your ingredients to a food processor and process your ingredients very well
7. Return the mixture to your Ninja Foodi pot and sauté for about 3 minutes
8. Ladle your soup in serving bowls
9. Serve and enjoy your soup!

Nutrition Information

Calories: 150| Fat: 7g | Carbohydrates: 15g | Fiber: 1 g |Protein: 5g

Recipe 51: Lentil and carrots Soup

TIME TO PREPARE
6 minutes

COOK TIME
25 Minutes

SERVING
4 People

Ingredients

- 2 Tablespoons of extra virgin olive oil
- 2 Teaspoons of ground cumin
- 1 Pinch of chili flakes
- 5 Cups of washed chopped carrots
- 1 and 1/2 cups of washed red lentils
- 1 Cup of vegetable stock
- 1/2 Cup of coconut milk
- 1 Spoon of plain Greek yogurt

Instructions

1. Start by frying the ground cumin and the chili flakes for about 2 minutes in your Ninja Foodi
2. Add a little bit of extra virgin olive oil with the carrots, the red lentils, the vegetable stock and the coconut milk
3. Close your Ninja Foodi and seal the valve
4. Set the timer to about 25 minutes and the pressure to High
5. When the time is up, turn off the heat and do a quick pressure release
6. Open the lid when it is safe to do it; then transfer your ingredients to a food processor and process it until it becomes smooth
7. Return the soup to the pressure cooker and if it is too thick, add ½ cup of stock to it and cook without a lid for about 2 and 3 minutes using the button SEAR/SAUTE
8. Season your soup with 1 pinch of salt and 1 pinch of ground black pepper
9. Serve and enjoy your delicious soup with plain Yogurt!

Nutrition Information

Calories: 110.4| Fat: 0g | Carbohydrates: 24g | Fiber: 6.4 g |Protein: 8g

Recipe 52: Mushroom Soup

TIME TO PREPARE
8 minutes

COOK TIME
25 Minutes

SERVING
4 People

Ingredients

- 1 Teaspoon of Olive Oil
- 2 Garlic cloves
- 1 to 2 Bay Leaves
- 8 to 10 Peppercorns
- 1 Large, roughly chopped potato
- 1 Pound of cleaned and chopped Mushrooms
- 1 Cup of Water
- 1 Cup of coconut Milk
- 1 Pinch of salt
- 1 Pinch of ground black pepper
- 1 Tablespoon of olive oil

Instructions

1. Pour the olive oil with the garlic, the bay leaf and the peppercorns in your Ninja Foodi Inner Pot
2. Sauté your ingredients for about 2 to 3 minutes; using the button "sear/sauté"
3. Add in the mushrooms, the potatoes, the water and the salt
4. Close the Ninja Foodi and set the timer for about 20 minutes and the pressure to High
5. When the time is up; turn off your Ninja Foodi and quick release the pressure
6. Transfer your soup to a blender and puree it very well
7. Return the mixture to your pressure cooker and add in the milk
8. Adjust the seasoning with 1 pinch of salt and 1 pinch of ground black pepper
9. Press the button "SEAR/SAUTE" then sauté for about 2 minutes
10. Ladle the soup in serving bowls
11. Serve and enjoy your soup with whole wheat bread!

Nutrition Information

Calories: 203| Fat: 13.6g | Carbohydrates: 15g | Fiber: 0.5 g |Protein: 6.1g

Recipe 53: Spicy Chili

TIME TO PREPARE
6 minutes

COOK TIME
20 Minutes

SERVING
3-4 People

Ingredients

- 1 Tablespoon of oil
- 1 Cup of chopped onion
- 1 Tablespoon of minced garlic
- 1 Pound of ground beef
- 1 Cup of canned fire-roasted finely chopped tomatoes
- 1 Tablespoon of canned chipotle chilies into adobo sauce
- 1 or 2 Corn tortillas
- 1/2 Cup of water
- 3 Teaspoons of Mexican red Chile powder
- 2 Teaspoons of ground cumin
- 2 Teaspoons of salt

Instructions

1. Heat your Ninja Foodi using the button "SEAR/SAUTE"
2. When the Ninja Foodi becomes hot, add in the oil and the chopped onions and the minced garlic and stir for about 30 seconds
3. Add in the ground beef and sauté for about 2 minutes
4. In the meantime, blend the chipotle chili, the canned tomatoes and the tortillas until it becomes smooth
5. Mix your spices all together in a bowl and combine it very well
6. Add the spices and sauté the mixture for about 30 seconds
7. Add in the corn tortillas and the tomatoes; then pour in about 1/2 cup of water over your ingredients
8. Lock the lid of your Ninja Foodi and make sure to seal the valve
9. Pressure cook for about 18 minutes
10. When the time is up, turn off the heat and naturally release the pressure
11. Carefully open the lid

- 1 Teaspoon of dried oregano

12. Serve and enjoy your chili!

Nutrition Information

Calories: 202| Fat: 6g | Carbohydrates: 17g | Fiber: 6 g |Protein: 19g

Recipe 54: Shrimp Stew

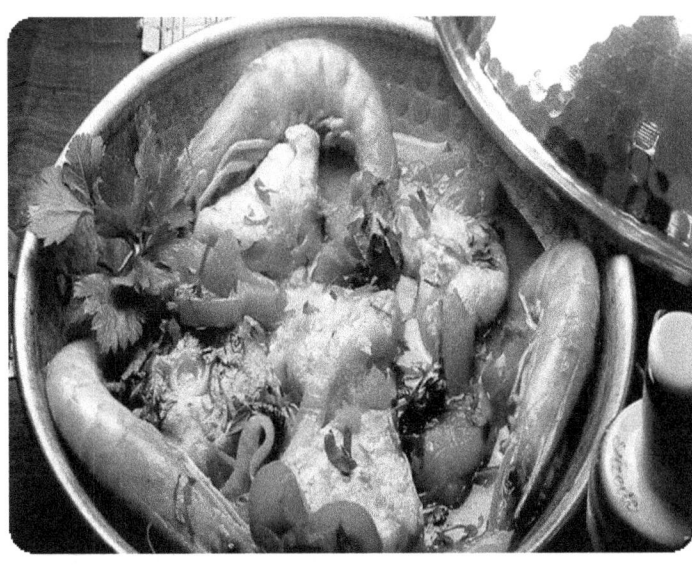

TIME TO PREPARE
7 minutes

COOK TIME
20 Minutes

SERVING
4 People

Ingredients

- 1 and 1/2 pounds of peeled and deveined raw shrimp
- 1/4 Cup of olive oil
- 1/4 Cup of diced onion
- 1 Minced garlic clove
- 1/4 Cup of diced roasted red pepper
- 1/4 Cup of chopped fresh cilantro
- 1 Can of 14 oz of diced tomatoes
- 1 Cup of coconut milk
- 2 Tablespoons of Sriracha hot sauce
- 2 Tablespoons of fresh lime juice
- 1 Pinch of salt
- 1 Pinch of ground black pepper

Instructions

1. Heat the olive oil in your Ninja Foodi and sauté the onions for about 2 minutes using the button "SEAR/SAUTE"
2. Add in the peppers and the garlic and cook for about 2 additional minutes
3. Add in the shrimp, the tomatoes and the cilantro and sauté for about 4 minutes
4. Add in the milk and the sriracha and close the lid of the Ninja Foodi
5. Set the timer to about 20 minutes and the pressure to High; make sure the valve is in sealed position
6. When the time is up, turn off your Nionja Foodi; then do a quick pressure release
7. Open the lid of the pressure cooker; then add in the lime juice
8. Season the stew with 1 pinch of salt and 1 pinch of pepper.
9. Garnish your soup with fresh cilantro
10. Serve and enjoy your Stew!

Nutrition Information

Calories: 237.5| Fat: 2.8g | Carbohydrates: 34.3g | Fiber: 3.2 g |Protein: 15.6g

Recipe 55: Quinoa Stew

TIME TO PREPARE
7 minutes

COOK TIME
20 Minutes

SERVING
3 People

Ingredients

- 1 Teaspoon of coconut oil
- 1 Medium, chopped yellow onion
- 2 Chopped celery stalks
- 3 Chopped carrots
- 4 Minced garlic cloves garlic
- 2 Seeded and finely chopped jalapeños
- 3 and ½ cups of water
- 1 Can of 28 ounces diced tomatoes
- 1 Can of 15 ounces of rinsed and drained black beans
- 1 and ½ teaspoons of ground cumin
- 2 Teaspoons of fine sea salt
- ½ Cup of dry quinoa
- ¼ Cup of chopped

Instructions

1. Warm the oil in your Ninja Foodi by pressing the setting function "SEAR/SAUTE"
2. Add in the onion, the carrots, the garlic, the celery and the jalapenos
3. Pour in the water, the tomatoes; the beans, the cumin, the salt and the quinoa and sauté for about 3 minutes
4. Season with 1 pinch of salt and 1 pinch of ground black pepper
5. Add the quinoa and close the lid of your Ninja Foodi and seal the lid
6. Pressure Cook for about 20 minutes
7. When the time is up; turn off the heat and quick release the pressure
8. When it is safe to do; open the lid of the Ninja Foodi
9. Transfer the quinoa mixture to a processor and puree the quinoa for about 30 seconds
10. Divide the mixture into serving bowls; then serve and enjoy your quinoa stew!

fresh cilantro
- ⅛ Teaspoon of cayenne pepper
- 1 Pinch of freshly ground black pepper
- Chopped cilantro
- Sliced lime and avocado

Nutrition Information

Calories: 110.4| Fat: 3g | Carbohydrates: 18g | Fiber: 2.9 g |Protein: 3g

CHAPTER 4: PASTA AND NOODLES RECIPES

Recipe 56: Shrimp Angel Pasta

TIME TO PREPARE
5 minutes

COOK TIME
10 Minutes

SERVING
4-5 People

Ingredients

- 1 and ¼ pounds of peeled and deveined shrimp
- 12 Oz of dry angel hair pasta
- 3 Tablespoons of olive oil
- 3 Tablespoons of coconut oil
- 1 Pinch of salt
- 1 Pinch of freshly ground black pepper
- 3 Minced garlic cloves
- 1 and ½ teaspoons of lemon zest
- 3 Tablespoons of fresh lemon juice
- 3 Tablespoons of chopped fresh basil
- 3 Tablespoons of chopped fresh parsley

Instructions

1. Start by boiling 2 cups of water in a large pan over a medium high heat
2. Add in the pasta and cook à la dente
3. Cook the pasta for about 5 minutes on a high heat
4. When the time is up, drain the pasta and reserve ½ cup of water aside
5. Spray your Ninja Foodi with cooking spray; then add in the shrimp, the salt and the pepper and sauté for about 2 minutes using the button SEAR/SAUTE
6. Toss in the drained pasta in with the shrimp and pour in 1/3 cup of the reserved water
7. Add in the lemon zest and the lemon juice
8. Sprinkle with parsley and basil
9. Season with 1 pinch of salt and 1 pinch of pepper
10. Serve and enjoy your delicious pasta!

- ½ Cup of finely shredded parmesan

Nutrition Information

Calories: 164.1| Fat: 7.9g | Carbohydrates: 14.9g | Fiber: 0.3 g |Protein: 10.1g

Recipe 57: Ground Beef Spaghetti

TIME TO PREPARE
5 minutes

COOK TIME
6 Minutes

SERVING
4 People

Ingredients

- 1 lb of ground beef
- 1 cup of chopped onion
- 1 and ½ tsp of sea salt
- 1 teaspoon of basil
- 1 tsp of Italian seasoning
- 1 Cup of chopped green peppers
- 1 Roasted garlic bulb, roast
- 1 tsp of sugar
- 1/8 to ¼ teaspoons of red pepper flakes
- 14.5 ounces of fire roasted tomatoes
- 4 cups of beef stock, divided
- 24 ounces of spaghetti sauce your favorite
- ½ Pound of spaghetti noodles; stacked and broken in half

Instructions

1. Set your Ninja Foodi to the function "sauté" to High; then add in 1 pound of ground beef, 1 and ½ teaspoons of fine grind sea salt; 1 teaspoon of dried basil; 1 teaspoon of Italian seasoning and about 1 cup of chopped onion to the inner pot
2. Break up the meat with a wooden utensil and stir for about 3 minutes
3. Add in 1 cup of diced green pepper or other veggies of your choice
4. Add in the whole bulb of roasted garlic with 1 teaspoon of white sugar
5. When the ground beef is perfectly cooked through, add in about one can of fire roasted tomatoes of about 14.5
6. Pour in 3 cups of beef broth; but don't stir
7. Pour in a jar of about 24 oz of your favorite spaghetti sauce. Pour the remaining cup of beef stock and place the lid back on
8. Shake the jar to remove the sauce from the sides; then pour into the pot and add in ¼ to ½ teaspoon of red pepper flakes
9. Break ½ pound of spaghetti noodles into half and;

- 6 Ounces of tomato paste

then gently push down the noodles

10. Add in a can of 6 oz of tomato oasta on top; but don't stir
11. Lock the lid of the Ninja Foodi and seal the valve; then set the timer to 3 minutes and the pressure to High
12. When the timer beeps; do a natural pressure release for 3 minutes and open the lid when it is safe to do it
13. Close the lid of the Tender Crisp and let sit for about 5 minutes
14. Top with cheese; then serve and enjoy your spaghetti!

Nutrition Information

Calories: 441| Fat: 16g | Carbohydrates: 50g | Fiber: 5g |Protein: 25g

Recipe 58: Cheesy Pasta

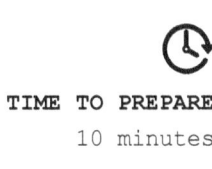

TIME TO PREPARE
10 minutes

COOK TIME
13 Minutes

SERVING
4 People

Ingredients

- 1 lb of spicy ground sausage
- 1 Finely diced onion
- 1 Jar of spaghetti sauce of about 24 oz.
- 2 Cups of water or of beef broth
- ¼ tsp of garlic salt
- ¼ teaspoon of salt
- 1 ½ cups of grated mozzarella cheese
- ½ cup of grated parmesan cheese
- 1 Finely diced green onion optional
- 2 Tablespoons of olive oil
- 8 Oz of spaghetti noodles ½ a regular size of about 16 oz; broken into thirds

Instructions

1. Press the button "Sauté" on your Ninja Foodi; then add in the olive oil; the diced onions, the salts and the ground sausage
2. Turn off the Ninja Foodi; then pour in the jar of spaghetti sauce. Then pour in 2 c. of water or broth into your jar. Put lid back on and shake to get out remaining sauce. Pour this liquid into your Ninja Foodi and stir
3. Break the noodles into thirds of equal size pieces; then sprinkle into your Ninja Foodi on top of the liquid.
4. Gently submerge with a spoon them into the liquid but make sure not to stir
5. Lock the Ninja Foodi with a lid and make sure the valve is in sealed position
6. Pressure cook for about 9 minutes at High pressure
7. When the timer beeps; do a quick pressure release; then remove the lid
8. Stir in 1 cup of mozzarella cheese until it melts; then sprinkle the remaining ½ cup of mozzarella cheese and the parmesan cheese until it melts over the top of the spaghetti
9. Add the diced green onions; then close the Ninja Foodi Air Crisp lid and Air Crisp using the button

"Air Crisp" for about 5 minutes
10. Serve and enjoy your pasta!

Nutrition Information

Calories: 333| Fat: 14g | Carbohydrates: 37g | Fiber: 3g |Protein: 16g

Recipe 59: Ninja Foodi Spicy Pepperoni Pasta with Cheese

TIME TO PREPARE
7 minutes

COOK TIME
6 Minutes

SERVING
3-4 People

Ingredients

- 1 Package of 12oz of Pasta
- 4 Cups of Water
- 1 Green or Red chopped bell Pepper
- ¼ Cup of chopped sweet onion
- ¼ Cup of sliced black Olives
- ½ Cup of thinly sliced Pepperoni
- A jar of about 14oz of Pizza Sauce
- A can of 8 oz of Tomato Sauce
- Grated Mozzarella or Italian Cheese

Instructions

1. In the pot of your Ninja Foodi; add in the pasta with the water.
2. Add in your remaining ingredients; but don't stir in the cheese and reserve it for the topping
3. Make sure the water is covering the pasta; but reserve the cheese for the topping and do not stir
4. Close the lid of your Ninja Foodi and seal the Valve
5. Pressure cook at a High pressure for about 6 minutes
6. Do a quick release pressure; then serve and enjoy your dish after topping it with cheese!

Nutrition Information

Calories: 273| Fat: 10g | Carbohydrates: 35g | Fiber: 5g |Protein: 11g

Recipe 60: Ninja Foodi Lasagne

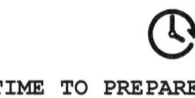

TIME TO PREPARE
15 minutes

COOK TIME
30 Minutes

SERVING
3-4 People

Ingredients

- 3 Cups of chopped veggies of your choice
- ½ Medium chopped Onion
- 2 Tablespoons of minced garlic
- 1 Tablespoon of olive oil
- 1 Cup of low fat ricotta cheese
- 1 Large egg
- 2 Cups of fresh spinach
- 2 Cups of tomato sauce
- 12 Uncooked whole grain lasagne noodles
- 1 Cup of shredded mozzarella cheese

Instructions

1. Boil 2 cups of water in a pan filled with water; and when the water starts boiling; add in the lasagna sheets and cook for about 2 minutes
2. Start by chopping the veggies; the sauté the garlic and the onion in a little bit of oil in your Ninja Foodi inner pot
3. Add the veggies to your Ninja Foodi and sauté the ingredients for 4 to 5 minutes using the SEAR/SAUTE; then set the ingredients aside
4. Combine the egg with the ricotta cheese in a bowl; then add in the fresh spinach and pour in a little bit of sauce in the bottom of a baking tray that fits your Ninja Foodi
5. Top the ingredients with the lasgna noodles; then pour in ½ cup of ricotta mixture, 1/half of the veggies, and about ¾ cup of the sauce.
6. Repeat the same process with the rest of the

noodles; the remaining quantity of sauce and the mozzarella cheese
7. Cover the baking tray with aluminium foil
8. Place a rack in a low position in your Ninja Foodi and place the tray over the rack; then close the lid
9. Press the button Bake/Roast and cook for about 25 to 30 minutes
10. When the time is up; turn off your Ninja Foodi and carefully remove the baking tray from the Ninja Foodi and remove the foil
11. Slice the lasagne, then serve and enjoy its delicious taste!

Nutrition Information

Calories: 440| Fat: 21.2g | Carbohydrates: 10.5g | Fiber: 0g |Protein: 25.1g

Recipe 61: Ninja Foodi Gnocchi

TIME TO PREPARE
10 minutes

COOK TIME
7 Minutes

SERVING
3 People

Ingredients

- 1 Cup of mashed potato flakes
- 1 Cup of boiling water
- 1 Lightly beaten egg
- 1 and ½ cups of all-purpose flour
- ½ Teaspoon of dried basil
- ¼ Teaspoon of garlic powder
- 1/8 Teaspoon of salt
- 1/8 Teaspoon of pepper
- 6 Cups of water
- 1 and ½ cups of Pasta sauce
- ½ Cup of grated Parmesan cheese

Instructions

1. Place the potato flakes into a large bowl
2. Add in the boiling water and add the egg; then sift in the flour and the seasonings
3. Knead the dough over a floured surface; then divide the dough into about 4 portions
4. Roll each of the dough portions into ropes; then cut the dough into pieces
5. Press the pieces with a floured fork
6. Pour 1 cup of water in Ninja Foodi and toss in the gnocchi
7. Lock the lid of your Ninja Foodi and set the timer to about 5 minutes on a HIGH pressure using the button "Pressure Cook"
8. When the timer beeps; quick release the pressure; then open the lid
9. Heat a little bit of oil in a large skillet and transfer the gnocchi to it and lightly fry it for about 1 to 2 minutes on both sides

10. Sprinkle a little bit of cheese over the gnocchi
11. Serve and enjoy your gnocchi with tomato sauce!

Nutrition Information

Calories: 254| Fat: 1.5g | Carbohydrates: 29g | Fiber: 2.6g |Protein: 7.7g

Recipe 62: Ninja Meatball Pasta

TIME TO PREPARE
7 minutes

COOK TIME
30 Minutes

SERVING
4 People

Ingredients

- 20 Frozen meatballs
- 1 lb of Pasta elbow or ziti.
- 32 Oz of your favorite jarred sauce
- 1 Jar of water
- 1 Cup of shredded cheese

Instructions

1. Using the Air Crisp basket of your Ninja Food; add in the meatballs to it
2. Pull down the crisping lid; then set to Air Crisper for about 18 minutes at a temperature of about 350°F
3. Check the meatballs throughout the cooking process
4. Remove the Air Crisp basket and set it aside
5. Add the jarred sauced; then fill the jar with water and add it to the Ninja Foodi
6. Add in any additional seasoning; then add rosemary and the Italian seasoning, you can add a little bit of rosemary and of Italian seasoning
7. You can add a splash of red wine to your prepared mixture; then add the pasta and lightly submerge
8. Close the lid of your Ninja Foodi; then set your Ninja Foodi to High pressure for about 6 minutes using the button "Pressure Cook"
9. Make sure the valve is in sealed position
10. Do a quick natural release for about 3 minutes; then do a quick release

11. Open the lid when it is safe to do it; then add the meatballs back in your ninja Foodi and top with the shredded cheese and Air Crisp on a temperature of 375°F for about 5 minutes
12. Serve and enjoy your pasta with Otalian bread and fresh parmigiana cheese!

Nutrition Information

Calories: 432| Fat: 14.1g | Carbohydrates: 52.2g | Fiber: 4.3g |Protein: 19.5g

Recipe 63: Ninja Foodi Chicken Ramen

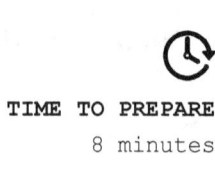

TIME TO PREPARE
8 minutes

COOK TIME
26 Minutes

SERVING
4 People

Ingredients

- 2 Pounds of bone-in, skin-on chicken thighs
- 1 Piece of about 1 inch of peeled ginger
- 4 Peeled and smashed garlic cloves
- ½ Peeled yellow onion
- ¼ Cup and 2 tablespoons of soy sauce, divided
- 5 Cups of water
- ¼ cup of Dijon mustard
- 1 Tablespoon of granulated sugar
- 4 Packages of about 3 ounces each of instant ramen noodles
- For the Toppings: Thinly sliced fresh scallions

Instructions

1. Place the ginger with the chicken, the garlic, the onion, ¼ cup of soy sauce, and the water in your Ninja Foodi
2. Stir your ingredients to mix very well; then close the lid and make sure the valve is in sealed position
3. Select the button "PRESSURE" and set the pressure to HIGH.
4. Set the timer to about 22 minutes; then select the button START/STOP to begin.
5. When the pressure time is up; quick release the pressure and move the valve to VENT position
6. Carefully remove the lid when the pressure cooking time is done
7. Remove the chicken; then place it in a large bowl to cool
8. Use a strainer to remove the garlic, the onion and the ginger and discard
9. When the chicken is cool to handle; remove the skin and shred the chicken meat; discard the bone
10. In a bowl; mix 2 tablespoons of soy sauce with the sugar
11. Combine the mixture with the shredded meat, then

- Soft boiled eggs and some nori sheets
- Corn and bamboo shoots
- Cooked veggies
- The zest of citrus

store the meat in a large bowl wrapped with a plastic wrap

12. Select the button "SEAR/SAUTÉ" and set to HIGH; then select the START/STOP to begin and bring the mixture to a Boil
13. Add the Dijon; then whisk
14. Press the button START/STOP to cancel the SEAR/SAUTÉ.
15. Ladle the noodles into bowls; then divide the broth among the bowls and cover each with a plastic wrap for about 3 to 4 minutes
16. Once the noodles become softened; remove the plastic wrap; then add the meat and the toppings
17. Serve and enjoy your dish with the meat and toppings!

Nutrition Information

Calories: 513| Fat: 13g | Carbohydrates: 57g | Fiber: 3g |Protein: 42g

Recipe 64: Vermicelli Rice Noodles

TIME TO PREPARE
8 minutes

COOK TIME
7 Minutes

SERVING
4 People

Ingredients

- 1 Tablespoon of garlic infused olive oil
- 1 tbsp of grated ginger
- 1 Finely diced red Chilli
- 1 Red pepper
- 2 Tablespoons of chopped fresh chives
- 1 Cup of sliced babycorn
- 1 Large handful of bean sprouts
- 1 Pound of vermicelli rice noodles
- 1 Medium julienne carrot
- 1 medium julienne courgette
- 1 Large handful of shredded spring greens
- 4 Teaspoons of low fod map curry powder
- ½ Tablespoon of

Instructions

1. Heat the Ninja Foodi to a Medium heat on the SEAR/SAUTE setting. Then add in the garlic oil
2. Add in the ginger and the chilli to the Ninja Foodi; then stir for about 1 minute
3. Add in the red pepper; the chives and the baby corn and stir-fry for about 3 additional minutes
4. Add in the beansprouts with 1 splash of water and sauté for about 2 additional minutes
5. Add in the curry powder and the maple syrup; then add in the noodles, the carrot, the courgette, the spring greens, the tamari and the lime juice
6. Stir your ingredients very well for about 1 minute
7. Top with coriander and lime wedges; then serve and enjoy your delicious pasta!

maple syrup
- 3 Tablespoons of tamari
- The juice of 1 lime

For garnishing:
- 2 lime wedges
- 1 to 2 tbsp of fresh chopped coriander

Nutrition Information

Calories: 368| Fat: 17g | Carbohydrates: 33g| Fiber: 4g |Protein: 22g

Recipe 65: Pasta Salad

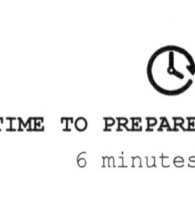

TIME TO PREPARE
6 minutes

COOK TIME
13 Minutes

SERVING
3-4 People

Ingredients

- 1 Box of about 16 ounces of elbow pasta
- 4 Cups of water
- 1 Tablespoon of kosher salt
- 2 Tablespoons of olive oil
- ½ Cup of finely diced red onion
- 1 Cup of thinly sliced roasted red pepper
- ¼ Cup of sliced black olives
- ½ Pound of 8 ounces of diced fresh mozzarella
- ½ Cup of chopped basil
- For the Red Wine Vinaigrette:
- 1 Box of 16 ounces of elbow pasta
- 4 cups of water
- 1 tablespoon of kosher

Instructions

1. Place the pasta, the water and the salt in the Ninja Foodi pot.
2. Assemble the pressure lid and make sure the pressure release valve is placed in SEAL position
3. Select the PRESSURE and set to HIGH. Then set the timer to about 3 minutes and select START/STOP to begin
4. While the pasta is cooking, prepare the wine vinaigrette; then combine the ingredients of the vinaigrette except for the olive oil; then slowly whisk on the oil and adjust to taste; then set aside
5. When the pressure cooking time is complete; do a natural pressure release for about 10 minutes ; then quick release any remaining pressure by moving the pressure release valve to VENT position
6. Carefully remove the lid
7. Remove the Ninja Foodi and strain the pasta in a colander
8. Transfer to a bowl in the refrigerator and let cool for about 20 minutes
9. Once cool; stir the red onion, the roasted peppers, the black olives, the mozzarella and the basil and

- salt
- 2 tablespoons of olive oil
- ½ cup of diced red onion
- 1 Cup of thinly sliced roasted red peppers
- ¼ Cup of sliced black olives
- ½ Pound of fresh diced mozzarella
- ½ Cup of chopped basil

add to the red wine vinaigrette
10. Serve and enjoy your dish!

Nutrition Information

Calories: 288| Fat: 10.8g | Carbohydrates: 42.4g| Fiber: 1.7g |Protein: 6.3g

Recipe 66: Ninja Foodi Cannelloni

TIME TO PREPARE
15 minutes

COOK TIME
22 Minutes

SERVING
5 People

Ingredients

- 9 tubes of cannelloni
- Three cups of Tomato Sauce
- 2 cups of Béchamel
- 2 tbsp of Parmesan cheese

For the filling:

- 1 pound of cooked spinach
- ½ Pound of ricotta
- 2 tbsp of Parmesan cheese
- 1 large beaten egg

Instructions

1. Pre-heat your Ninja Foodi using the setting function "SEAR/SAUTE"
2. Combine the ingredients of the filling.
3. Season the comp with the salt and the black pepper
4. Boil 1 cup of water in a medium pan and add the cannelloni tubes when it starts boiling; then cook for about 2 minutes
5. Discard the cannelloni tubes and drain very well; then let cool down for 5 minutes
6. Spoon the mixture into the cannelloni tubes.
7. Place your cannelloni tubes into a buttered dish
8. Spoon the tomato sauce and the Béchamel sauce over the cannelloni.
9. Sprinkle with the cheese.
10. Place the tray in the Ninja Foodi and close the lid
11. Press the button BAKE/ROAST and set the timer to about 20 minutes and the temperature to about 350°F
12. When the timer beeps; serve and enjoy your delicious cannelloni!

Nutrition Information

Calories: 517| Fat: 15.6g | Carbohydrates: 71.2| Fiber: 6.3g |Protein: 24.9g

Recipe 67: Ninja Foodi Pepperoni Pasta

TIME TO PREPARE
10 minutes

COOK TIME
22 Minutes

SERVING
4-5 People

Ingredients

- 1 lb of Itallian Sausage
- 1 Finely diced large onion
- 1 teaspoon of kosher salt
- ½ teaspoon of dried oregano
- ½ Teaspoon of dried basil
- ¼ Teaspoon of ground black pepper
- ¼ Teaspoon of crushed red pepper
- 6 Finely minced large garlic cloves
- 1 Cup of red wine
- 1 Can of 28 ounces of peeled San Marzano tomatoes
- 1 Can of 28 ounces of San Marzano tomato

Instructions

1. Select the button function Sear/Saute MD:Hi on your Ninja Foodi; let preheat for about 5 minutes; then cook the sausage for about 5 minutes
2. Add the onion and the olive oil to the Ninja Foodi and sauté for about 2 minutes
3. Add the salt, the oregano, the basil, the black pepper, and the crushed red pepper; then stir for about 5 minutes
4. Add the browned sausage; the garlic and the wine; then add in the tomatoes, the tomato puree, the chicken stock and the pasta to the Ninja Foodi and stir
5. Lock the lid of the Ninja Foodi in place; then select the button "High Pressure" and set the timer for about 6 minutes and press the button Start
6. When the pressure cooking time is complete, do a natural pressure release for about 10 minutes; then carefully remove the lid
7. Stir your sauce with a wooden spoon; then crush the tomatoes
8. Cover your pasta mixture with about 3 cups of shredded mozzarella.
9. Lay the pepperoni slices across the mozzarella.

puree
- 2 Cups of chicken stock
- 1 Box of 16 ounces of dry rigatoni pasta
- 4 Cups of shredded mozzarella cheese divided
- 1 Package of 6 ounces of thinly sliced pepperoni

10. Sprinkle the remaining mozzarella over the pepperoni slices.
11. Close the crisping lid; then select the button "Air Crisp" and set the temperature to about 400°F and set the time to about 5 minutes.
12. Select the Start to begin the cooking process
13. Serve and enjoy once the cooking time is over

Nutrition Information

Calories: 465| Fat: 25g | Carbohydrates: 29| Fiber: 3g |Protein: 26g

Recipe 68: Ninja Foodi Fettuccini

TIME TO PREPARE
8 minutes

COOK TIME
25 Minutes

SERVING
3-4 People

Ingredients

- 1 Tablespoon of olive oil
- ½ Teaspoon of salt
- ¼ Teaspoon of black pepper
- 2 to 3 chicken breasts
- 2 Tablespoon of salted butter
- 2 Tablespoons of minced garlic
- 2 Cups of heavy cream
- 2 Cans of 14.5 oz of chicken broth
- 1 Pound of dried fettuccine noodles
- ½ Cup of grated parmesan cheese
- ½ Freshly shredded parmesan cheese
- 2 Cups of fresh chopped broccoli

Instructions

1. Turn the Ninja Foodi on the function sauté
2. Add in the oil
3. Season the chicken breasts with 1 pinch of salt and 1 pinch of pepper; then add to the hot Ninja Foodi
4. Brown the chicken breasts on each side for about 2 minutes per side
5. Once the chicken breasts are browned, remove it from the Ninja Foodi and set it to use it later
6. Add the butter and the garlic to your Ninja Foodi and stir; make sure to scrape the bottom with a plastic spatula
7. Once the butter is melted, you can add in the cream and heat until it stars simmering
8. Pour in the chicken broth and the salt and stir
9. Break the pasta into half over the Ninja Foodi and add in to the sauce mixture.
10. Stir so that the pasta is covered in sauce; but don't over stir
11. Place the brown chicken breasts on top of the pasta and the sauce
12. Place the pressure cooker lid on your Ninja Foodi and sauce; then press the button High pressure and cook for about 10 minutes or just enough that the

all pasta is covered in sauce. Do not over stir
13. Place browned chicken breasts on top of pasta and sauce
14. Place pressure cooker lid on Ninja Foodi and cook on high pressure for about 10 minutes. Make sure the valve is in "seal" position
15. When the timer beeps, do a natural pressure release for about 6 to 8 minutes; then slowly move the valve to the button "Release"
16. Continue with a quick release method to release any remaining pressure; then remove the lid when it is safe to do it
17. Remove the chicken breasts from the Ninja Foodi; then add in the cheese and the raw broccoli and stir very well
18. While the broccoli is still "steaming" in the hot pasta and the cheese sauce, shred the chicken on tip and return to your Ninja Foodi
19. Stir; then serve and enjoy your Fettuccini!

Nutrition Information

Calories: 192| Fat: 1.6g | Carbohydrates: 36| Fiber: 2.4g |Protein: 7.2g

Recipe 69: Beef Wellington

TIME TO PREPARE
10 minutes

COOK TIME
25 Minutes

SERVING
4-5People

Ingredients

- 1 Tablespoon of cooking oil spray
- 1 Pound of beef fillet
- 1 Chopped small onion
- ½ Pound of finely chopped chestnut mushrooms
- 1 Crushed garlic clove
- 3 Tablespoon of brandy
- 1 Tablespoon of balsamic vinegar
- 1 Teaspoon of cornflour
- 1 Pound of light puff pastry sheet
- 1 Beaten egg

Instructions

1. Place your Ninja Foodi using the button "SEAR/SAUTE" and pour in 2 cups of water
2. Place a rack in the bottom of your Ninja Foodi
3. Line a baking tray with a baking paper; then grease the tray with vegetable oil
4. Brown the beef in a large skillet with a little bit of olive oil and sauté it for a few minutes
5. Spray the skillet with more oil and brown the onion for about 4 minutes
6. Add in the mushrooms and the garlic and stir-fry it for about 6 minutes
7. Add the brandy and the vinegar and cook for about 7 minutes
8. Remove the skillet from the heat and add in the corn flour
9. Lay a pastry sheet over the baking tray and brush it with a little bit of the egg
10. Spread half the quantity of the mushroom mixture into the middle of one of the wellington pastry
11. Place the beef over the top of the spinach mixture

- 1 Teaspoon of poppy seeds
- 1 Pound of steamed snap peas
- 2 Pounds of mashed potatoes

and press it very well
12. Fold the mixture of the meat and fold the pastry over the uncovered part of the pastry; then pinch both ends to form a shape of parcel
13. Trim any excess of pastry; then brush the top with an egg and sprinkle over poppy seeds
14. Place the wellington in a baking tray lined with a parchment paper and cover it with a sheet of aluminium foil
15. Put the baking tray over the steel rack in your Ninja Foodi
16. Close the lid of your Ninja Foodi and seal it very well
17. Press the button "BAKE/ROAST" and bake the wellington for about 25 minutes
18. When the time is up; turn off your Ninja Foodi and do a quick release pressure; then open the lid and carefully remove the tray from your Ninja Foodi
19. Slice the wellington; then serve and enjoy your delicious dinner with steamed snap peas and mashed potatoes!

Nutrition Information

Calories: 626| Fat: 40g | Carbohydrates: 43| Fiber: 2g |Protein: 26g

Recipe 70: Tuna Fusilli

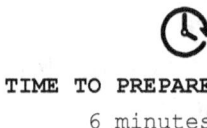

TIME TO PREPARE
6 minutes

COOK TIME
10 Minutes

SERVING
4 People

Ingredients

- 4 tbsp of Filippo Berio
- 2 tbsp of olive oil
- 3 cups of tomato sauce
- ½ teaspoon of chilli flakes
- Zest of ½ a lemon
- 500g of Fusilli pasta
- 120g of a can of drained tuna

Instructions

1. Turn on your Ninja Foodi and press the button "SEAR/SAUTE"
2. Add in the tomato sauce and heat it for tomato sauce in Ninja Foodi.
3. Now stir in the chilli flakes and sauté for around 5 minutes.
4. Meanwhile, boil the water and cook your pasta for around 10 minutes.
5. Flake your tuna in your tomato sauce
6. Add the lemon zest and let boil for about 5 minutes
7. Drain the pasta and drain it in the sauce of the tuna.
8. Now, place the pasta in a tray and place it in your Ninja Foodi
9. Lock the lid and press the button "BAKE/ROAST" and bake for about 5 minutes
10. When the time is up; turn off your Ninja Foodi; then open the lid
11. Enjoy your delicious!

Nutrition Information

Calories: 295| Fat: 13g | Carbohydrates: 31g| Fiber: 4g |Protein: 12g

Recipe 71: Ninja Foodi Mac and Cheese

TIME TO PREPARE
6 minutes

COOK TIME
10 Minutes

SERVING
5 People

Ingredients

- 1 lb of Ditalini pasta or elbow macaroni
- 3 Cups of shredded cheese Gouda, Parmesan and mozzarella cheese
- 3 Cups of chicken broth
- 1 Cup of Water
- 1 Pinch of salt and 1 pinch of Pepper to taste
- ½ Stick of melted butter
- 1 Cup of Breadcrumbs or panko
- ½ Cup of Bacon bits

Instructions

1. First add in the chicken broth, the water and the pasta.
2. Stir your ingredients evenly; then set the Ninja Foodi
3. Low Pressure Cook for about 10 minutes.
4. It will take about 7 minutes to come to pressure
5. Naturally release the pressure for about 10 minutes
6. Release the steam that is left; then open the lid
7. Add in 3 cups of cheese; the salt; the pepper and the garlic salt
8. Mix your ingredients very well; then melt the butter in a microwave.
9. Add in one cup of bread crumbs and the melted butter to a bowl.
10. Mix your ingredients very well; then spread over the macaroni and cheese in the Ninja Foodi and sprinkle with bacon bits right on top
11. Serve and enjoy your pasta!

Nutrition Information

Calories: 461| Fat: 23g | Carbohydrates: 42g| Fiber: 2.2g |Protein: 12g

Recipe 72: Stuffed Pasta Shells with cheese and tomato sauce

TIME TO PREPARE
12 minutes

COOK TIME
25 Minutes

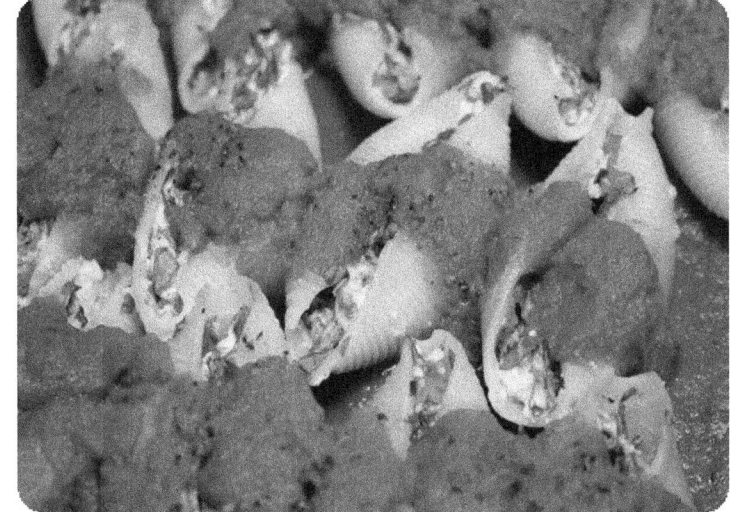

SERVING
5 People

Ingredients

- 1 package of jumbo pasta shells
- 2 large beaten eggs
- 2 cups of ricotta cheese
- 1 lb of shredded mozzarella cheese
- 1 cup of grated Parmesan cheese
- 1tbsp of dried parsley
- 2 tbsp of salt
- 1 tbsp of ground black pepper
- 3 cups of pasta sauce
- One can of sliced and fresh mushrooms

Instructions

1. Preheat your Ninja Foodi by pressing the setting function "SEAR/SAUTE"
2. Pour the water in the Ninja Foodi and wait until it starts boiling
3. Add in the pasta to the boiling water and add a pinch of salt
4. Close the Pressure cooker lid of the Ninja Foodi and set the timer to about 4 to 5 minutes
5. Set the pressure to High; make sure the valve is in sealed position
6. Once the timer beeps, do a quick release pressure; then open the lid when it is safe to do it; drain the pasta and set it aside.
7. In a deep large bowl, combine the eggs, the ricotta; and half the quantity of the mozzarella.
8. Add half the quantity of the Parmesan
9. Add the parsley, the salt and the pepper until everything is well combined.
10. Stuff the cooked shells with the mixture of the ricotta and place it in a tray.
11. Place the tray in your Ninja Foodi after cleaning it and lock the lid in place; then press the button BAKE/ROAST for about 10 minutes at a

temperature of 350°
12. In a large deep bowl; stir your pasta sauce with the mushrooms, the mozzarella and the Parmesan.
13. Now, take the shells out of your Ninja Foodi.
14. In the same cooking tray, pour the sauce over your stuffed shells.
15. Return the baking tray to the Ninja Foodi and lock the lid; then cook for about 10 minutes
16. When the time is off, serve and enjoy your pasta shells.

Nutrition Information

Calories: 180| Fat: 4g | Carbohydrates: 26g| Fiber: 1g |Protein: 9g

Recipe 73: Seafood Pasta

TIME TO PREPARE
5 minutes

COOK TIME
10 Minutes

SERVING
4 People

Ingredients

- 1 tbsp of olive oil
- 1 chopped onion
- 1 chopped garlic clove
- 1 tbsp of paprika
- 1-lb can of tomatoes (Cubed)
- 4 cups of chicken stock
- 1 Pound of broken spaghetti
- ½ pound-pack of frozen and defrosted seafood mixture
- 1 Pinch of chopped parsley leaves
- Lemon wedges

Instructions

1. Heat the oil in your Ninja Foodi by pressing the button "SEAR/SAUTE"
2. Add in the onions and the garlic; and sauté for 4 minutes.
3. Add the paprika and the tomatoes.
4. Pour in the stock and let simer for about 3 minutes
5. Add in the pasta and close the lid of your Ninja Foodi
6. Place the pressure cooker lid on; then set the timer for about 3 minutes and the pressure to High; make sure the valve is in sealed position
7. When timer beeps; do a quick release pressure; then open the lid when it is safe to do it
8. Add in the seafood and press the setting button "SEAR/SAUTE" and sauté for about 3 to 4 minutes.
9. Serve and enjoy your pasta dish!

Nutrition Information

Calories: 197| Fat: 5.3g | Carbohydrates: 33.1g| Fiber: 0.8g |Protein: 11.2g

Recipe 74: Pasta Bolognese

TIME TO PREPARE
6 minutes

COOK TIME
14 Minutes

SERVING
3-4 People

Ingredients

- 1 Pound of your favorite pasta
- 3 Cups of Bolognese sauce
- 2 Cups of shredded mozzarella cheese
- Water
- 1 pinch of salt
- Flaked of dried parsley flakes.

Instructions

1. Pour the water in your Ninja Foodi
2. Press the button "SEAR/SAUTE"; then when it starts boiling; add in the pasta and a little bit of salt
3. Close the lid of your Ninja Foodi and seal the valve
4. Set the timer to about 4 minutes and the pressure to High
5. When the timer beeps; turn off your Ninja Foodi; do a quick pressure release
6. Open the lid when it is safe to do it; then drain the pasta and combine it with the Bolognese sauce in a large bowl
7. Put the pasta in a cooking tray.
8. Top the pasta with shredded cheese.
9. Place the tray on a low rack in your Ninja Foodi and set to BAKE/ROAST
10. Set your timer to 10 minutes.
11. After the timer sets off, serve and en and enjoy your pasta and don't forget to garnish it with parsley!

Nutrition Information

Calories: 151| Fat: 11.3g | Carbohydrates: 3.1g| Fiber: 0.6g |Protein: 10.6g

Recipe 75: Ninja Foodi Picadillo

TIME TO PREPARE
6 minutes

COOK TIME
20 Minutes

SERVING
3-4 People

Ingredients

For the Sauté:
- 2 lbs of Ground Beef
- 2 Tbsp of Olive Oil
- 1 Diced Yellow Onion
- 1 Finely diced Green Bell Pepper
- 4 Finely diced garlic

For the Pressure Cooking:
- 1 Cup of Beef Broth
- 1 Can of 8 oz of tomato sauce
- 1 Can of 6 oz of tomato paste
- ¼ Cup of white Wine Vinegar*
- 10 Roughly chopped,

Instructions

1. Set your Foodi's sauté function to HI while you are preparing your vegetables.
2. Add in the olive oil to your Ninja Foodi pot and once hot, add in the onion and the bell pepper.
3. Cook for about 6 to 8 minutes; then add in the garlic and cook for about 30 to 60 seconds
4. Add in the ground beef and cook for about 5 minutes
5. Add in the cooking ingredients and stir very well; then seal the lid and cook on HI for about 6 to 8 minutes
6. When the time is up, turn off the Ninja Foodi and do a quick release pressure by turning the valve to Venting position
7. Open the lid when it is safe to do; then stir in 1 to 2 tablespoons of chopped cilantro
8. Serve and enjoy the Picadillo!

Jalapeño Stuffed Olives
- 2 Oz of raisins
- ½ Tablespoon of Cumin
- 1 Teaspoon of dried Oregano
- 1 Pinch of salt and 1 pinch of pepper, to taste

Nutrition Information

Calories: 200| Fat: 7.3g | Carbohydrates: 13.1g| Fiber: 1.7g |Protein: 21.3g

CHAPTER 5: STAPLE RECIPES

Recipe 76: Mushroom Risotto

TIME TO PREPARE
5 minutes

COOK TIME
10 Minutes

SERVING
3-4 People

Ingredients

- 4 Ounces of Wild or porcini dried Mushrooms
- 8 Oz of fresh and roughly chopped Cremini Mushrooms
- 1 Tablespoon of olive oil
- 1 Tablespoon of Extra Virgin Olive Oil
- 1 and ½ cups of brown or Arborio Rice
- 3 Large chopped Shallots
- 1 Teaspoon of Fennel Seeds
- ½ Cup of dry White Wine
- 2 Cups of Chicken Broth
- 1 and ½ cups of

Instructions

1. Place the dried mushrooms of dried Mushrooms in about 2 cups of boiling water and let tenderize for about 10 minutes
2. With a slotted spoon; transfer the mushrooms to a cutting board and coarsely chop it
3. Reserve the soaking liquid aside; then
4. Turn your Ninja Foodi on by pressing the button "SEAR/SAUTE"; then add in the olive oil and add the rice, the shallots and the fennel seeds
5. Sauté your ingredients for about 3 minutes
6. Add rice, the shallots and fennel seeds and stir for about three minutes.
7. Add the wine and cook your ingredients until the wine almost evaporates; make sure to stir from time to time
8. Pour in the Chicken Stock; the mushrooms and the salt
9. Lock the lid of the Ninja Foodi and seal the Valve; then cook on a high heat for about 10 minutes
10. When the time is up; turn off your Ninja Foodi and quick release the pressure
11. Open the lid of your Ninja Foodi and stir the rice

- Mushroom water
- ½ Teaspoon of sea salt
- 1 Cup of 3 oz of Asiago Cheese
- 2 Tablespoons of chopped Flat Leaf Parsley

until it becomes creamy
12. You can add more liquid if the rice is too thick
13. Mix in the cheese and the parsley and season the Risotto with 1 pinch of pepper and little bit of cider vinegar
14. Serve and enjoy your risotto!

Nutrition Information

Calories: 435| Fat: 17.1g | Carbohydrates: 56.5g| Fiber: 4.2g |Protein: 11.3g

Recipe 77: Ninja Foodi Stuffed Okra

TIME TO PREPARE
6 minutes

COOK TIME
20 Minutes

SERVING
4 People

Ingredients

- 1 Pound of okra
- 1 Tablespoon of red chilli powder
- 1 Tablespoon of cumin
- 1 Teaspoon of coriander powder
- 3 Tablespoon of coarsely ground roasted peanuts
- 1/8 Teaspoon of turmeric
- 1 Tablespoon of cooking oil
- 1 Pinch of salt
- Finely chopped cilantro

Instructions

1. Wash the okra and dry it; then cut the top and the bottom of the okra
2. Make vertical slits over each of the okras and make sure not to split the okra into halves
3. Prepare the stuffing by mixing the ground peanuts, the red chilli powder, the turmeric, the cumin, the coriander powder, the fresh cilantro and the salt
4. Fill each of the okras with the prepared filling
5. Add a little bit of oil in your Ninja Foodi
6. Arrange the okra in the bottom of your Ninja Foodi cooker and arrange the okras
7. Pour 1 cup of water in your Ninja Foodi
8. Close the lid of your Ninja Foodi and make sure to seal the valve
9. Pressure cook for about 20 minutes on High pressure
10. When the time is up; turn off your Ninja Foodi; then quick release the pressure when the time is up
11. Open the lid when it is safe to do it
12. Remove the lid of your Ninja Foodi; then serve and enjoy your delicious dish!

Nutrition Information

Calories: 182.1| Fat: 13g | Carbohydrates: 17.3g| Fiber: 5g |Protein: 4g

Recipe 78: Ninja foodi Donuts

TIME TO PREPARE
10 minutes

COOK TIME
15 Minutes

SERVING
7 People

Ingredients

- 2 tbsp of butter
- ½ Cup of sugar
- 2 and ¼ cup of plain flour
- 1 and ½ teaspoons of baking powder
- 1 teaspoon of salt
- 2 beaten egg yolks
- ½ Cup of sour cream
- 1 cup of melted butter
- Use Cinnamon Sugar
- 1/3 Cup of caster sugar
- 1 teaspoon of cinnamon

Instructions

1. In a deep bowl, press all together the quantity of butter and the sugar until the mixture becomes crumbly.
2. Add the egg yolk and keep stirring until the yolks become very smooth and well combined.
3. Add the quantity of flour, the baking powder and the salt into another bowl.
4. Add around 1/3 of flour and half of the sour cream.
5. When the mixture is very well combined, sift in 1/3 of your flour, then 1/2 of the sour cream.
6. Now, the last step is to stir the sour cream.
7. In the fridge, place the mixture at the same time you are preparing the bench by spreading flour on the surface.
8. Roll-out your dough to make it into dough of 1cm of thickness.
9. Cut the dough into small circles, and then create the shape of a donut.
10. Now, preheat your Ninja Foodi using the button

BAKE/ROAST at a temperature of about 320°F
11. Use the melted butter and using a brush, rub the doughnuts on both sides of each donut with the mixture.
12. Arrange the donuts in a greased tray; then place the tray in your Ninja Foodi and lock the lid
13. Set the timer to 15 minutes and the temperature to 350°F using the button "BAKE/ROAST"
14. Once cooked, open the lid of your Ninja Foodi; then rub the donuts again with butter and dip it this time in the cinnamon sugar.
15. Serve and enjoy your donuts.

Nutrition Information

Calories: 225.7| Fat: 13g | Carbohydrates: 24.5g| Fiber: 0.9g |Protein: 2.8g

Recipe 79: Ninja Foodi Biscuits

TIME TO PREPARE
5 minutes

COOK TIME
9 Minutes

SERVING
8-9 People

Ingredients

- 1 Can of 12 oz of buttermilk biscuits
- Oil to use for spraying
- A little bit of Cinnamon sugar for coating

Instructions

1. With the help of a small biscuit cutter, try to cut a hole out of each of your biscuits.
2. Spray the two sides of your biscuit and place it in your Ninja Foodi Air Crisp basket in one single layer then close your Ninja Foodi and slide it into your Ninja Foodi
3. Press the button "Air Crisp" and cook for about 5 minutes
4. When the cooking time is complete, open your basket
5. Turn your biscuits and spray oil on them and return them back to the Air Crisp basket; then close the lid of the Ninja Foodi
6. Set your timer for around 4 minutes.
7. When the cooking time is finished, open your Ninja Foodi and remove the biscuits, then sprinkle with the cinnamon sugar while the biscuits are still hot
8. Repeat the same process with the rest of the biscuits
9. Serve and enjoy your biscuits!

Nutrition Information

Calories: 260.3| Fat: 8.5g | Carbohydrates: 41.5g| Fiber: 1g |Protein: 4.8g

Recipe 80: Butter Fingers

TIME TO PREPARE
5 minutes

COOK TIME
6 Minutes

SERVING
10 People

Ingredients

- 2 ½ cups of all-purpose flour
- ¾ cup of granulated sugar
- ½ lb of butter, (around 2 sticks)
- 1 teaspoon of vanilla
- 1 16oz. box of confectioner's sugar

Instructions

1. In a deep and large bowl, combine all your ingredients except for the confectioner's sugar.
2. Now, roll the mixture into tiny "fingers" or you can roll it into balls if you prefer balls.
3. The next step is to place your balls into batches in your Air Crisp basket, and be careful not to overcrowd the Air Crisp basket
4. Close the lid of your Ninja Foodi and Air Crisp for about 6 minutes
5. When the cooking time is finished, turn off your Ninja Foodi; then transfer the butter fingers to a serving platter
6. Sprinkle the sugar over the butter fingers or you can sprinkle with almonds
7. Serve with coffee and tea and enjoy!

Nutrition Information

Calories: 190| Fat: 7g | Carbohydrates: 29g| Fiber: 1g |Protein: 2g

Recipe 81: Peach Cake

TIME TO PREPARE
5 minutes

COOK TIME
20 Minutes

SERVING
4-5 People

Ingredients

- 2 cups of canned peaches
- 1 box of white cake mix
- ¼ Cup of butter
- 1 ½ cup of Lemon lime soda

Instructions

1. Preheat your Ninja Foodi by pressing the button "ROAST/BAKE"
2. Drain the juice of the cans of peach (Using the frozen peaches are the best here).
3. In a baking tray, sift your box of white cake mix above the peaches.
4. Cut around ¼ cup of warm butter into very small pieces.
5. Take the lime of the lemon soda and pour around ½ over the batter
6. Try not to leave dry spots and cover all the batter
7. Place the tray in your Ninja Foodi
8. Set the timer to about 20 minutes by pressing the button "Air Crisp"
9. Once cooked, open the lid of your Ninja Foodi; then remove the tray from the Ninja Foodi and let it chill for about 3 minutes
10. Serve and enjoy your delicious peach cake

Nutrition Information

Calories: 432| Fat: 14g | Carbohydrates: 76g| Fiber: 2g |Protein: 22g

Recipe 82: Pineapple Cobbler

TIME TO PREPARE
5 minutes

COOK TIME
10 Minutes

SERVING
3 People

Ingredients

- ½ Cup of butter
- 1 Cup of milk
- 1 Can of drained pineapple chunks
- ½ Cup of brown sugar
- 1 jar of halved maraschino cherries

Instructions

1. Preheat your Ninja Foodi by to 390° F.
2. Take a baking tray that fits your Ninja Foodi
3. Grease the tray with butter; then take a large bowl and sift the flour in it.
4. Add the sugar and the milk; then mix very well until the mixture becomes smooth
5. Pour the batter into your greased pan.
6. In another bowl, toss the pineapple with the brown sugar until the fruit becomes well coated. Drop the pineapple mixture into the batter.
7. Sprinkle the mixture with your cherries.
8. Place the baking tray in your Ninja Foodi and lock the lid
9. Press the button "ROAST/BAKE" and bake for about 10 minutes and the temperature to 350°F
10. When the time is up; turn off your Ninja Foodi
11. Serve and enjoy your Pineapple cobbler!

Nutrition Information

Calories: 414| Fat: 9.98g | Carbohydrates: 79.7g| Fiber: 1.3g |Protein: 4.32g

Recipe 83: Ninja Foodi Bluberry Cobbler

TIME TO PREPARE
7 minutes

COOK TIME
20 Minutes

SERVING
4 People

Ingredients

- 1 Cup of all-purpose flour
- 1 and ½ cups of divided white sugar
- 1 Teaspoon of baking powder
- ½ Teaspoon of salt
- 6 Tbsp of cold butter
- ¼ Cup of boiling water
- 2 Tbsp of cornstarch
- ¼ Cup of cold water
- 1 Tbsp of lemon juice
- 4 Cups of fresh rinsed and drained blackberries

Instructions

1. Preheat your Ninja Foodi to 390° F by pressing the button "BAKE/ROAST"
2. Line one baking sheet using an aluminum foil.
3. In a deep and large bowl, combine all together the flour
4. Add ½ cup of sugar
5. Add the baking powder and the salt.
6. Cut the mixture of the butter until your mixture starts to resemble the coarse crumbs.
7. Stir in around ¼ cup of boiling water
8. Keep stirring until your mixture becomes moist.
9. In another separate bowl, start by dissolving the quantity of cornstarch in the cold water.
10. Mix in the remaining 1 cup of sugar, the lemon juice, and the blackberries.
11. Transfer the mixture to a baking pan and boil your ingredients.
12. Boil the ingredients together, keep stirring consistently.
13. Drop the dough into your baking pan gradually.
14. Place your baking pan over the foil lined baking sheet

15. Place the baking tray in your Ninja Foodi Foodi and lock the lid
16. Press the button "BAKE/ROAST" and bake for about 20 minutes in the preheated Ninja Foodi
17. Once the timer beeps; turn off your Ninja Foodi; then remove the tray from the Ninja Foodi and set it aside to cool for about 15 minutes
1. Serve and enjoy your cobbler!

Nutrition Information

Calories: 290.5| Fat: 8.4g | Carbohydrates: 51.1g| Fiber: 3.6g |Protein: 4.7g

Recipe 84: Caramel Cobbler

TIME TO PREPARE
10 minutes

COOK TIME
22 Minutes

SERVING
10 People

Ingredients

- 1 Cup of butter
- 2 and ¼ Cups of brown sugar
- 1 Cup of light corn syrup
- 1 Can of sweetened condensed milk
- 1 Teaspoon of vanilla extract
- 1 Tbsp of chocolate
- 1 lb of milk chocolate
- 1 Tbsp of butter

Instructions

1. Grease a baking pan that fits to your Ninja Foodi
2. In saucepan, melt the butter over a low heat
3. Add the brown sugar and the corn syrup
4. Add the milk and keep stirring
5. After 5 minutes; remove the saucepan from the heat
6. Add the vanilla extract
7. Preheat your Ninja Foodi to a temperature of about 250°F
8. Pour the mixture that you have prepared into a baking tray
9. Place the tray in your Ninja Foodi and lock the lid
10. Press the button "BAKE/ROAST" and bake for about 22 minutes
11. When the timer beeps; turn off your Ninja Foodi, and open the lid of your Ninja Foodi
12. Let cool for 20 minutes; then cut into squares
13. Let the caramel squares chill in the refrigerator until it becomes firm.
14. Melt the chocolate by adding to it 1 tbsp of butter to the top of bowl in your microwave.
15. Finally, dip the caramel squares in the chocolate

and place it in the paper of wax to chill
16. After a few minutes, serve and enjoy!

Nutrition Information

Calories: 130| Fat: 3g | Carbohydrates: 26g| Fiber: 1g |Protein: 1g

Recipe 85: Marshmallow Pudding

TIME TO PREPARE
5 minutes

COOK TIME
25 Minutes

SERVING
4 People

Ingredients

- 2½ Cups of heavy cream
- ¾ Cup of sugar
- 5 medium eggs
- ½ Teaspoon of kosher salt
- 1 teaspoon of fresh lemon juice
- 1 teaspoon of pure vanilla extract
- 5 Cut croissants into 1 inch each cube.
- ¼ Cup of chocolate chips
- ½ Cup of mini marshmallows

Instructions

1. With the help of a blender, combine all together the cream, the sugar, the eggs, the salt, the lemon juice and the vanilla extract.
2. Purée the ingredients until they become smooth.
3. Put your croissant cubes into the Air Crisp Basket of your Ninaj Foodi
4. Close the lid and set the timer to about 4 to 5 minutes
5. Press the button "Air Crisp" and once the cubes are toasted, turn off the Ninja Foodi and transfer the cubes to the mixture of the custard in order to soak.
6. Spray a baking pan with a non-stick spray
7. Now, add the mixture of the custard with chocolate chips and add the marshmallows to mix; then ingredients all together
8. Now, put your baking pan in your Ninja Foodi and

close the lid

9. Press the button "BAKE/ROAST" and bake for about 20 minutes at a temperature of 340°F
10. When the timer beeps; serve and enjoy with a cream of your choice!

Nutrition Information

Calories: 90.2| Fat: 0.3g | Carbohydrates: 23.2g| Fiber: 0.4g |Protein: 0.7g

Recipe 86: Ninja Foodi Scones

TIME TO PREPARE
10 minutes

COOK TIME
15 Minutes

SERVING
6 People

Ingredients

- 2 Cups of plain flour
- 4 Tbsp of baking powder
- 2 Tbsp of sugar
- 1 Pinch of salt
- 4 Tbsp of margarine
- 1 Cup of milk
- 1 Cup of dates

Instructions

1. Preheat your Ninja Foodi to 390°F usin,g the button "BAKE/ROAST"
2. Sift the flour and add the baking powder to it into a large bowl.
3. Now, add the sugar and the salt.
4. Add the margarine with your fingers into your mixture.
5. Combine the milk and the dried fruits
6. You should obtain stiff dough
7. Out of the dough, make around 11 to 12 ball shapes.
8. Flatten the balls and arrange them in a greased baking pan.
9. Place the pan in your Ninja Foodi and close the lid
10. Set the timer for about 15 minutes and bake your scones.
11. Once the timer sets off, open the lid of your Ninja Foodi
12. Serve and enjoy your scones.

Nutrition Information

Calories: 490| Fat: 23g | Carbohydrates: 64g| Fiber: 2g |Protein: 7g

Recipe 87: Ninja Foodi Pikelets

TIME TO PREPARE
6 minutes

COOK TIME
10 Minutes

SERVING
3 People

Ingredients

- 1 Cup of flour
- 1 Teaspoon of baking powder
- 1 Large egg
- ¼ Cup of sugar
- ¾ Cup of milk

Instructions

1. In a large bowl, sift in the flour and the baking powder.
2. In a separate bowl, beat all together the eggs and the sugar until they become thick.
3. Add your egg and the mixture of the sugar.
4. Pour in the milk to the quantity of flour and mix it until it all combined together.
5. Evenly pour the batter into greased ramekins; make sure the poured mixture is thin.
6. Arrange the ramekins in the AAir Crisp Basket of your Ninja Foodi and slide the Air Crisp basket in the Nina Foodi
7. Close the lid of the Ninja Foodi; then bake for about 7 minutes
1. When your pikelets are baked, open the lid; then serve and enjoy with honey, chocolate or jam of your choice.

Nutrition Information

Calories: 120| Fat: 3g | Carbohydrates: 0g| Fiber: 0g |Protein: 1g

Recipe 88: Anzac Biscuits

TIME TO PREPARE
5 minutes

COOK TIME
6 Minutes

SERVING
8 People

Ingredients

- 1 Cup of flour
- 1 Teaspoon of baking powder
- 1 Large egg
- ¼ Cup of sugar
- ¾ Cup of milk

Instructions

1. Pre-heat your Ninja Foodi to 360° F using the button "BAKE/ROAST"
2. Mix all together the flour
3. Add the baking powder, the coconut and the rolled oats
4. Add the sugar and keep mixing.
5. Melt the quantity of margarine; then add the honey or the syrup.
6. Mix your dry ingredients and mix it with your wet ingredients.
7. Dissolve your baking soda into the warm water.
8. Mix the soda powder with the rest of the ingredients.
9. Use both your hands in order to roll into quietly small balls.
10. Place your balls in a greased baking pan
11. Arrange the balls into the tray and flatten the balls slightly with the use of a fork.
12. Place the tray in your Ninja Foodi; then bake for about 15 minutes
13. Once the timer sets off, remove the baking dish from the Ninja Foodi
14. After 5 minutes, serve and enjoy your biscuit!

Nutrition Information

Calories: 123| Fat: 5g | Carbohydrates: 16g| Fiber: 5g |Protein: 1g

Recipe 89: Chocolate Madeleine

TIME TO PREPARE
5 minutes

COOK TIME
20 Minutes

SERVING
3-4 People

Ingredients

- ¼ Cup of sifted all-purpose flour
- ¼ Cup of unsweetened cocoa powder
- ½ Teaspoon of baking powder
- 1 Pinch of salt
- ½ Cup of butter
- ½ Teaspoon of vanilla extract
- ¼ Cup of white sugar
- 1 Large egg
- 2 Egg yolks
- 1/3 Cup of confectioners' sugar

Instructions

1. Preheat your Ninja Foodi by pressing the button "BAKE/ROAST"
2. In a large bowl, mix all together the flour, the cocoa, the baking powder and the salt.
3. Cream your butter using the vanilla together with the sugar.
4. Add one egg and the yolk; keep beating until the mixture becomes smooth.
5. Butter a Madeleine baking dish.
6. Stir in your dry ingredients until they become totally combined only.
7. Put teaspoons of your batter into your Madeleine shell shapes.
8. Place the Madeleine baking tray with the Madeline in it in your Ninja Foodi and close the lid
9. Bake the Madeleine for about 15 minutes
10. Once the timer beeps, remove the Madeleine from the Ninja Foodi
11. Serve and enjoy your Madeline when it cools up
12. Sprinkle with white sugar
13. Serve and enjoy your Madeleine.

Nutrition Information

Calories: 290| Fat: 15g | Carbohydrates: 36g| Fiber: 1g |Protein: 3g

Recipe 90: Snow balls

TIME TO PREPARE
10 minutes

COOK TIME
12 Minutes

SERVING
8 People

Ingredients

- 1 Cup of butter
- ½ Cup of confectioners' sugar
- ¼ Teaspoon of salt
- 1 Teaspoon of vanilla extract
- 2 1/4 Cups of all-purpose flour
- 1 Cup of chopped pecans
- 1/3 Cup of confectioners' sugar for dusting it
- 1/4 Cup of crushed peppermint candy canes

Instructions

1. Preheat your Ninja Foodi by pressing the button "BAKE/ROAST"
2. Grease a baking tray with butter
3. Add in ½ cup of the confectioners' sugar; then add in the vanilla.
4. Mix the flour with the pecans and the salt.
5. Roll around a tablespoon or two of your batter into a number of small balls; then place it over a cookie sheet and place the sheet in the baking tray
6. Place the baking tray in your Ninja Foodi; and bake your cookies in the preheated Ninja Foodi until for about 12 minutes using the button "BAKE/ROAST"
7. Once the timer goes off, remove the cookies from the Ninja Foodi
8. While the cookies are still hot, roll the cookies into confectioner's sugar.
9. Let cool for about Serve and enjoy your cookies!

Nutrition Information

Calories: 151| Fat: 9g | Carbohydrates: 16g| Fiber: 0g |Protein: 2g

Recipe 91: Palmier Biscuits

TIME TO PREPARE
7 minutes

COOK TIME
15 Minutes

SERVING
8 People

Ingredients

- 1 lb pack of frozen puff pastry
- 5 Tbsp of vanilla sugar
- 1 large egg white

Instructions

1. Defrost your pastry and roll it out into 2 rectangles (20x3)
2. Brush every piece of the pastry with the use of one egg white.
3. Sprinkle with white sugar.
4. Place each of the pastries over each other.
5. Roll each of the two pastries over the two sides to the middle of the pastries
6. Cut your roll into very thin slices and dip in the sugar vanilla.
7. Place the pastry into the Air Crisp Basket of your Ninja Foodi
8. Close the lid of your Ninja Foodi and press the button "BAKE/ROAST" and bake for about 15 minutes at a temperature of 370°F
9. When the timer beeps; turn off your Ninja Foodi; then serve and enjoy

Nutrition Information

Calories: 109| Fat: 6.21g | Carbohydrates: 12.21g| Fiber: 0.2g |Protein: 1.1g

Recipe 92: Ninja Foodi Croissant

TIME TO PREPARE
10 minutes

COOK TIME
30 Minutes

SERVING
6 People

Ingredients

- 1 ½ cups of white flour
- 2 Tbsp of dry yeast
- ½ Cup of milk
- 1/3 Cup of sugar
- ½ Cup of butter
- 1 pinch of salt
- 1 large egg
- ½ grated zest of lemon
- A little of butter to grease the baking dish

Instructions

1. Start by sifting the flour into a large bowl.
2. Add 1/3 cup of sugar
3. Add the butter, the lemon zest, the egg and the salt.
4. Now, dissolve your yeast in the warm milk
5. Add the mixture into the remaining ingredients and knead your smooth dough.
6. Set the dough aside in a warm place for 1 hour.
7. Cut the dough into around 3 pieces of the same size.
8. Make each roll of 30 cm and plait your rolls so that you can make a loaf
9. Place your loaves over in the Air Crisp Basket of your Ninja Foodi
10. Lock the lid of your Ninja Foodi and press the button "BAKE/ROAST" at a temperature of about 350°F for about 30 minutes
11. Serve and enjoy your delicious croissants!

Nutrition Information

Calories: 272| Fat: 14g | Carbohydrates: 13.3g| Fiber: 1.7g |Protein: 5.5g

Recipe 93: CATUCINI BISCUITS

TIME TO PREPARE
6 minutes

COOK TIME
18 Minutes

SERVING
4 People

Ingredients

- ½ Cup of plain flour
- 1 Teaspoon of baking powder
- 1 Cup of sugar
- 1 Pinch of salt
- 2 Eggs
- 2 Egg yolks
- ½ Cup of almonds
- ¼ cup of ground almonds
- Milk to use for coating
- Butter
- 1 Tablespoons of Flour for dusting the tray

Instructions

1. Preheat your Ninja Foodi to about 390° F by pressing the button "BAKE/ROAST"
2. Mix all of your ingredients and knead it into a dough
3. Form your dough into a shape of rolls; then brush it using milk.
4. Place the dough over a greased and floured baking tray.
5. Place the tray in your Ninja Foodi; then close the lid and set the temperature to 390° F
6. Set the timer to 18 minutes
7. When the timer sets off, remove the biscuits from the Ninja Foodiand set it aside to cool
8. After 5 minutes, cut your biscuits into slices; serve and enjoy!

Nutrition Information:

Calories: 138| Fat: 5.7g| Carbohydrates: 19g| Fiber: 1g |Protein: 3g

Recipe 94: Cocoa-Dusted Biscuits

TIME TO PREPARE
10 minutes

COOK TIME
22 Minutes

SERVING
8 People

Ingredients

- 2 cups of all purpose flour
- ½ Cup of caster sugar
- 1 Egg yolk
- 1 Pinch of salt
- 1 Cup of butter
- 1 Tbsp of cocoa powder
- 1 Egg white
- Butter
- Flour

Instructions

1. Preheat your Ninja Foodi to about 350°F; using the button "BAKE/ROAST"
2. Combine the flour with the sugar, the salt, the egg yolk and the butter in order to make sweet dough.
3. Knead the powder of the cocoa into 1 half of pastry and then put the halves in the refrigerator for 30 minutes.
4. Roll the pieces of your pastry to a thickness of 0.5 cm rectangle.
5. Brush your pastry using the egg white and then lay the piece of the chocolate over the top.
6. Roll your pastry and cut it into slices.
7. Now, arrange the dough in the Air Crisp basket of your Ninja Foodi
8. Close the lid of your Ninja Foodi and set at a temperature of 350°F
9. Bake the biscuits for about 20 minutes.
10. When the timer is off; open the lid of your Ninja Foodi; then remove the biscuits from the Air Crisp Basket
11. Serve and enjoy with tea or coffee!

Nutrition Information

Calories: 261| Fat: 20g | Carbohydrates: 18g| Fiber: 1g |Protein: 3g

Recipe 95: Cherry Soufflé

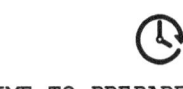

TIME TO PREPARE
5 minutes

COOK TIME
20 Minutes

SERVING
3 People

Ingredients

- 1lb of cherries
- ½ cup of butter
- 1 cup of sugar
- 3 egg yolks
- 1 pinch of salt
- ½ of lemon Juice
- ½ of corn flour
- 1 lb of low fat quark
- 3 egg whites
- ½ cup of flaked butter
- ¼ Cup of flaked almonds
- Butter to grease the baking pan

Instructions

1. Preheat your Ninja Foodi to a temperature of about to 350° F
2. Take a soufflé baking dish and grease it with butter
3. Now, in a deep and large bowl, beat the quantity of butter, the sugar, the egg, the yolks, the salt, the lemon juice, the corn flour and the quark until the mixture becomes fluffy.
4. Beat your egg whites until it becomes stiff and add it to the mixture
5. Take the greased baking dish, place the cherries on its bottom, and pour the mixture over it.
6. Top your soufflé with the flakes of butter and the almonds.
7. Place the baking tray in your Ninja Foodi and bake for about 20 minutes; using the button "BAKE/ROAST"
8. Open the lid of your Ninja Foodi; then let cool for 5 minutes
9. Serve and enjoy your soufflé!

Nutrition Information

Calories: 231.7| Fat: 3.8g | Carbohydrates: 28.8g| Fiber: 4.3g |Protein: 20.4g

Recipe 96: Ninja Foodi Tiramisu

TIME TO PREPARE
5 minutes

COOK TIME
6 Minutes

SERVING
4 People

Ingredients

- 1 pack of Amaretti biscuits
- 1/2 cup of strong black Café direct
- 2 Sloshes of amaretto liqueur
- 2 cups of mascarpone cheese
- 2 ½ cup of whipped double cream
- 1/2 teaspoon of vanilla essence
- Use icing sugar to taste
- ½ cup of cocoa powder in order to use it for dusting

Instructions

1. Crush you biscuits and layer it at the bottom of a baking dish.
2. Pour the coffee and the amaretto over the mixture.
3. In another bowl, mix all together, the mascarpone cheese.
4. Add the whipped cream, and add more amaretto
5. Add the vanilla extract until the mixture becomes very well blended.
6. Now place the baking tray in your Ninja Foodi and close the lid
7. Using the baking option, press the button "BAKE/ROAST" and bake for about 6 minutes in your Ninja Foodi
8. Once the timer sets off, remove the baking tray from the Ninja Foodi.
9. Place it in the refrigerator and after around 10 minutes; dust it with cocoa for 2 hours.
10. Serve and enjoy!

Nutrition Information

Calories: 492| Fat: 31.7g | Carbohydrates: 42.47g| Fiber: 1.6 g |Protein: 8.3g

Recipe 97: Rolled Oats and carrots bars

TIME TO PREPARE
10 minutes

COOK TIME
20 Minutes

SERVING
7 People

Ingredients

- 1 cup of honey
- 1 cup of peanut butter
- 3 ½ cups of rolled oats
- ½ cup of raisins
- ½ cup of grated carrot
- ½ cup of coconut

Instructions

1. Peel your carrots and grate it.
2. Place the honey together with the peanut butter in your Ninja Foodi and press the button "SEAR/SAUTE"
3. Cook the mixture for about 5 minutes
4. Now, add the oatmeal, the raisins, the carrots, and the coconut to your Ninja Foodi.
5. Keep stirring; then preheat your Ninja Foodi to a temperature of 350°F using the button "BAKE/ROAST"
6. Now, pour the mixture in a baking pan that fits your Ninja Foodi
10. Press your mixture into the bottom of the baking tray.
11. Bake in the Ninja Foodi with the lid closed for about 20 minutes.
12. When the time is up; turn off your Ninja Foodi
13. Cut into about 24 bars; then serve enjoy!

Nutrition Information

Calories: 297.4| Fat: 6.6g | Carbohydrates: 52.1g| Fiber: 7.3g |Protein: 11.8g

Recipe 98: Fruit Tart

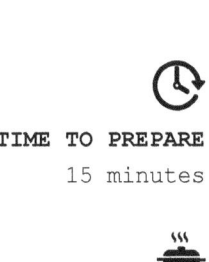

TIME TO PREPARE
15 minutes

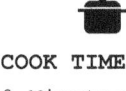

COOK TIME
30 Minutes

SERVING
6 People

Ingredients

- 1 stick about ½ cup of butter, to room temperature
- 1 and ¼ cups of flour, plus more for dusting
- ½ cup of granulated sugar
- 3 Tablespoons of cold water
- 1 Container of about 8 ounces of whipped cream cheese
- 1 Cup of frozen whipped topping, thawed
- ½ Cup of powdered sugar
- 1 and ½ cups of fresh mixed berries
- ½ Cup of red current preserves, melted

Instructions

1. In a stand mixer with a paddle attachment, whisk the butter until it becomes fluffy.
2. Add the flour on a low speed; then add the granulated sugar and ix until combined
3. Slowly add in cold water to form a ball.
4. Remove the dough; then place it a plastic wrap and refrigerate for about 1 hour
5. Whisk the cream and place in a plastic wrap. Refrigerate for about 1 hour; then in a mixing bowl, whisk all together the cream cheese, the whipped topping, and the powdered sugar until it becomes smooth and set aside.
6. Close the crisping lid; and preheat the Ninja Foodi by selecting the "BAKE/ROAST" setting the temperature to about 325°F, and the time to about 5 minutes.
7. Select the button START/STOP to start and while preheating your Ninja Foodi; lightly grease the

multi-purpose tray

8. Place the dough over a floured surface; then roll into a circle of about 9-inch.
9. Lay the dough into the greased pan and press it down evenly, with about ¼ inch of dough coming up of the sides of the pan.
10. Cover the dough with a parchment paper; then lay the pie weights or the dried beans over a parchment paper.
11. When your Ninja Foodi is preheated, place the pan on a reversible rack, making sure the rack is in the lower position; then place the rack with the pan in the pot.
12. Close the crisping lid; then select the "BAKE/ROAST" and set the temperature to about 325°F, and set the time to about 30 minutes.
13. Select the button START/STOP to begin and after 15 minutes, open the crisping lid and remove the weights or the beans and the parchment paper
14. Close the crisping lid to resume the cooking process
15. When the crust is golden; let cool;then remove the pan when it becomes cool to handle and with a spatula; spread the cream cheese over the crust and top with the berries and brush with the preserves and refrigerate for about 10 minutes
16. Slice, serve and enjoy!

Nutrition Information

Calories: 150| Fat: 12g | Carbohydrates: 12g| Fiber: 0.0g |Protein: 3g

Recipe 99: Stuffed Baked Apples

TIME TO PREPARE
6 minutes

COOK TIME
5 Minutes

SERVING
6 People

Ingredients

- 6 apple, around 6.5 oz per apple; cored out
- 3 Tablespoons of salted butter
- ½ Tablespoon of apple pie seasoning
- 1/3 Cup of brown sugar
- 1 Cup of water
- ¾ Cup of whole grain oats

Instructions

1. Rinse the apples; then pat dry, and with a pairing knife; make a round incision into the top of the stem
2. Scoop the middle of the apple and the seeds out so that you make room for the oat and sugar filling
3. In a large bowl; mix the oats with the apple pie seasoning and the brown sugar; then pour the melted butter into the mixture and stir
4. Fill the inside of the cored apples with 2 tablespoons of oat mixture
5. Pour the water into your Ninja Foodi Pressure cooker insert; and place a trivet into the bottom of your Ninja Foodi
6. Arrange the stuffed apples into your Ninja Foodi
7. Close your Ninja Foodi lid and seal the valve; then set to "Pressure Cook" at High for about 5 minutes and do a quick release when it is done
8. Carefully use the tongs to remove each of the apples and transfer to a platter.
9. You can put cinnamon on top or a swirl of whipped cream or ice cream

Nutrition Information

Calories: 155.9| Fat: 6.7g | Carbohydrates: 26.1g| Fiber: 2.2g |Protein: 1.1g

Recipe 100: Crumbled Apple

TIME TO PREPARE
10 minutes

COOK TIME
23 Minutes

SERVING
4 People

Ingredients

- Granny Smith apples (850g), cored, peeled and chopped into 2cm chunks
- 1 1/2 tbsp cornflour
- 180ml water, divided
- 1 tsp fresh lemon juice
- 3 tbsp granulated sugar
- Topping
- 75g plain flour
- 50g rolled oats
- 50g brown sugar
- 2 tbsp granulated sugar
- 100g unsalted butter
- 1 tsp ground cinnamon
- 1/4 tsp fine sea salt
- For Serving
- Vanilla ice cream

Instructions

1. Put the apples into your Multi-Purpose Pan; then in a large bowl; then stir 60ml of water with the corn flour, the lemon juice, and the sugar and toss very well with the apples.
2. Place the baking tray on the Reversible Rack and make sure it is on low position and cover the pan with a foil
3. Pour 120 ml of water into your Ninja Foodi and add in the rack; then assemble the pressure lid and make sure the valve is in SEAL position
4. Select the button "PRESSURE" and set your Ninja Foodi to HIGH; then set the time to 8 minutes using the button "START/STOP" to begin.
5. In a separate bowl, combine all the topping ingredients until it is very well incorporated.
6. When the pressure cooking is complete, quick release the pressure by turning the pressure release valve to the VENT position
7. Carefully remove the lid; then open when it is safe to do it
8. Remove the foil; then spread the topping on top and close the Air Crisp lid; using the button "AIR CRISP"; then set the time to about 10 minutes

9. Select the button "START/STOP" to begin the cooking process
10. Set the timer for about 10 minutes and the temperature to 360°F
11. You can rotate halfway through the cooking time; then cover with aluminum Foil to prevent any browning and cook for about 5 additional minutes
12. When the cooking time is complete, remove the rack with the pan from your Nina Foodi
13. Serve and enjoy your crumbled apples with vanilla ice-cream!

Nutrition Information

Calories: 275.1| Fat: 6.7g | Carbohydrates: 60.8g| Fiber: 5.1g |Protein: 2.8g

CONCLUSION

Not only Ninja Foodi can deliver you some of the most delicious results that you can ever taste, but Ninja Foodie is also a versatile cooking appliance that would make a great addition to any kitchen. Ninja Foodies is also easy-to use and easy to program it. And thanks to its dishwasher-safe accessories, Ninja Foodies are easy to clean and don't need so much space.

Generally, in terms of performance, Ninja Foodies can offer you a crispy taste thanks to its Tender crisp Technology and the taste will still be tender from the inside. So welcome to the amazing world of cooking using Ninja Goodies, that combines both the speed of quick crisping action of an air Fryer and the pressure cooking at the same time.

And with this official Ninja Foodi Cookbook for both beginners and professionals, you can maximize your multi-cooking appliance by whipping lots of flavourful delicious recipes all in one.

From beef, to back ribs and different types of poultry recipes to breads and desserts, you will find a large array of mesmerizing recipes that you won't be able to resist preparing again once you taste it. This comprehensive cookbook has made sure to include all the information you need to know about the use basics and different benefits of Ninja Foodies, so that you don't have any doubt once you decide to purchase a Ninja Foodi.

And no matter what you want to cook, this book includes various recipes that are suitable for different occasions and everyday meals as well. The pleasing recipes you will find included in this book are perfectly made for cooking at the touch of only one button, from different types of meats, soups, stews and delicious pasta recipes.

Besides, you will find a chapter of some of the most delicious and unexpected recipes that you will like Breads, cheesecakes and delicious desserts. Make your cooking experience easier and better with this must-have cookbook for any owner of multi-cooker whether you are a beginner or a master of using Ninja Foodies.

The revolutionary phenomenon, that is known as multifunctional electric cooker is able to steam, pressure cook, slow cook, sauté and pressure cook. And the combination of both steam and pressure cooks can help you obtain amazing pressure cooked dishes with a tender taste from the inside and a crispy taste from the outside in a short time. And this cooking appliance is perfect to use for busy and active families; besides it is a miraculous energy and time saver.

Thank you for Reading "the Ninja Foodi Pressure Cooker Cookbook"

We are proud to offer you this Ninja Foodi, Electric Pressure Cooker and Air Fryer cookbook and we hope that you enjoyed it. Please, don't hesitate to share this cookbook with your friends or to whomever you care about. We care about you and your health and we have tried to offer you an exciting cooking journey. And our dear readers; remember that we are always looking forward to any suggestions that will help us continue our work.